HEALERS
VERSUS
STEALERS

How to Outsmart the Thief in Your Dental Practice

DAVID HARRIS

Tellwell Talent
www.tellwell.ca

ISBN
978-1-77941-015-3 (Paperback)
978-1-77941-016-0 (eBook)

Table of Contents

Acknowledgments

Every day I am grateful to be able to work with the dedicated and talented group of investigators and support staff at Prosperident. The skills and determination they all bring to our work and the comfort they offer to our clients are immeasurable.

I would particularly like to thank Prosperident's Management Team of Kathy Kirkby, Jacob Hiltz, Sheilagh O'Driscoll, and Hailey Irvine for their enormous contributions to making Prosperident the formidable organization that it is today.

Many of the new concepts introduced in this book were developed as part of our Prosperident Webinar series that started in 2020. This series was the brainchild of Supervising Proactive Advisor Amber Weber-Gonzales. Amber, along with Supervising Examiner Wendy Askins, and Chief Communications Officer Sheilagh O'Driscoll have contributed many hours to putting on a great webinar series and developing many of the concepts and materials that you will find in this book.

I'd like to thank one of our most talented investigators, Supervising Examiner Scott Clifford, for helping develop the financial oversight concepts in Chapter 17.

I am also grateful to many people in the dental consulting community who have helped me along the way. In particular, I'd like to thank the *grand dame* of practice management consulting, Linda Miles, who believed in me early in my career and provided support in the way that only Linda can. Linda has helped many people in the consulting world, and I am privileged to be in that group.

I'd also like to acknowledge dental speaking mentor Vanessa Emerson. Vanessa's gently dispensed advice (which sometimes took me considerable time to follow) has always been 100% right.

Consultant and friend Janice Hurley took the cover picture and showed me the value of a professional and polished image.

Dr. Pam Maragliano-Muniz, editor of Dental Economics has been a tremendous friend and supporter and I am grateful for the interest she has shown in this topic.

And finally, consultants Sandy Baird, Kristin Pelletier, and Jennifer Schultz have been some of the best friends anyone could ask for. We have shared laughter often, tears occasionally, and the barriers of distance, time, and busy lives do not diminish the remarkable friendship we have enjoyed.

To all of you, my heartfelt thanks.

1

The Most Embezzled Profession

Dentistry is the most embezzled profession in North America. While embezzlement exists in every industry and profession and has existed ever since humans developed concepts of wealth and money, it seems to have a particular affinity for dentistry.

What is embezzlement? Embezzlement happens when someone who has been placed in a position of trust uses that trust to steal. In the dental context, embezzlement is most frequently committed by an employee, but the perpetrator might also be a business partner, associate dentist, consultant, accountant, or bookkeeper.

I'll discuss the reasons later but for now let me give you some stark numbers; the American Dental Association Council on Dental Practice published results of a 2019 survey of almost 20,000 of its members. We'll refer to this survey in this book as the "2019 CDP Survey." The 2019 CDP Survey found that over 48% of the dentists responding reported that they have been embezzled, with about half of those being victimized more than once.[1] We will discuss the 2019 CDP Survey in more detail in Chapter 21, but for now, let's just accept that this is a mainstream problem and not something that affects a small corner of the dental profession.

My best guess is that 70% of dentists will be afflicted with embezzlement at some point in their careers. Calling embezzlement a "pandemic" is not a stretch.

While sometimes the dollar amounts are jaw-dropping and at other times are insignificant, monetary losses only tell part of the story. Embezzlement victims and their remaining teams spend countless hours trying to determine what happened and remediate the mess that embezzlement makes of their records. Victims also suffer emotionally. Dentists who have been stolen from tell me about their trust issues, disturbed sleep patterns, and even relationship issues that all stem from the embezzlement that they experienced. Embezzlement has even been the trigger for some to sell their practices and revert to a purely clinical role.[2]

The goal of this book is simple – to equip practice owners and those who work with them with the tools to combat this scourge. We will start by digging into why embezzlement happens and the enabling factors that can increase the

---

[1]   American Dental Association. (2019). 2018 CDP Survey on Employee Theft in the Dental Practice. *Center for Dental Practice*

[2]   To hear one dentist tell his story about how embezzlement caused him to lose his desire for practice ownership, watch our webinar here - https://www.prosperident.com/why-justice-matters/

likelihood or "intensity" of theft and in later chapters will turn the conversation to helping practice owners develop the systems and habits that will protect them.

We will also discuss how to deal with embezzlement when it happens – we will tell you how to take a statement if a thief wants to confess, discuss interacting with law enforcement and your insurance company, and provide information on the various pitfalls you encounter. If you bought this book because you are now dealing with active embezzlement, you might want to start your reading at Chapter 24. And then go back to the beginning to help avoid being victimized again in the future.

If now or somewhere in this journey you become concerned about your practice or would like our assistance with putting better systems in place, we are happy to hear from you. You can call us at 888-398-2327 or contact us through our website at www.prosperident.com for a confidential conversation.

2

Why?

When the notorious 20th-century bank robber Willie Sutton was asked once why he robbed banks, Sutton thought the answer to this question was an obvious one. His simple explanation was, "Because that is where the money is."[3]

It is tempting to explain embezzlement in the same way; thieves embezzle "because they can." While most practices do present juicy targets for would-be embezzlers, not every staff member faced with such an opportunity chooses to steal, and we need a better framework for distinguishing those who would steal in a given situation from those who would not.

Probably the most oft-cited explanatory framework for embezzlement is the "Fraud Triangle" developed in the 1970s by criminologist Donald Cressey.[4] Cressey's Fraud Triangle suggests

---

[3]   Willie Sutton reference
[4]   Cressey, Donald R. *Other People's Money; a Study in the Social Psychology of Embezzlement.* Montclair, NJ: Patterson Smith, 1973

that there are three preconditions for embezzlement: pressure, opportunity, and rationalization. We will discuss Cressey's Fraud Triangle more fully in Chapter 4.

Although Cressey's model has considerable intuitive appeal, it is often misapplied by people citing it. This framework was intended to be descriptive as opposed to predictive, and it cannot satisfactorily address the question of differential behaviors by people facing the same stimuli. In a situation where two people both face pressure and comparable opportunity and have equal ability to rationalize their conduct, why does one of them steal but the other does not?

The other issue with Cressey's framework is that it has the potential to send people in the wrong directions. As mentioned, the Fraud Triangle has three preconditions. Two of them, pressure and rationalization, exist solely inside the head of the embezzler and therefore are not readily controllable by their employer. It is only the third factor, opportunity, that can be influenced by a practice owner, and intuitively reducing opportunity should reduce vulnerability. Several consultants writing on the topic have even described embezzlement as a "crime of opportunity." I profoundly disagree with this; embezzlement is a highly premeditative crime and there is little evidence of impulsive decisions to embezzle.

Much of the literature written for dentists on controlling embezzlement centers around nibbling away at the opportunity available to a thief. For example, many pundits suggest that getting insurance companies to pay a dentist via direct deposits instead of by check is a means of lessening embezzlement risk. (For more on why I no longer think that being paid by electronic funds transfer is a good idea, please see the discussion in Chapter 16.) Having the practice owner or spouse personally make bank deposits is another common recommendation.

But here is the issue with "denial of opportunity" strategies. Let's assume that you can get 100% of your incoming insurance payments delivered to you by electronic funds transfer. And let's also (falsely) assume that there is no way for a creative thief to hijack these payments. You will still receive at least 20-30% of your revenue from over-the-counter patient payments. And for a thief who will probably steal 2-4% of your collections, there is plenty of opportunity to scratch their larcenous itch from within these over-the-counter payments.

While this concept isn't intuitive, opportunity is a binary variable; either it exists for a given employee or it does not, and opportunity exists for most dental office employees to steal. Reducing but not eliminating opportunity does not change the likelihood that embezzlement will occur; it merely shapes how it will take place.

Resistance

The explanatory framework that I prefer to use when assessing the likelihood that someone will steal focuses on something I call "resistance" as the differentiating characteristic. Resistance is the degree of someone's unwillingness to break the rules while under some pressure to do so. Resistance can vary widely between people and can even vary for the same person over time.

Picture a group of 20 dieters being locked in the same room with a refrigerator full of delicious food and you will understand resistance. Some people will visit the fridge immediately or after waiting a short period. Others will rationalize ("I have lost three pounds this month and can treat myself"). Some will make it competitive – they will want to secure their food supply before everyone else empties the refrigerator. Others will try to "earn" a visit to the refrigerator by exercising, and others will just use willpower to hold out.

However, even that last steadfast group will eventually succumb to temptation if left in the room long enough as hunger takes hold.

Embezzlement is no different. Some will steal at the drop of a hat (zero-resistance employees). People who have exhibited criminal behavior in the past are among those whom we can expect to embezzle on very little pretext.

Others have some level of resistance but manage to rationalize their way around that resistance easily, and some are convinced that they "deserve" what they steal.

And even for the group with the strongest resistance, in sufficiently dire circumstances, they will overcome their resistance to stealing. For example, if someone in their family needs unaffordable life-saving surgery, this might be a situation when even those with strong resistance might entertain stealing as the solution.

What does resistance mean to your practice?

Zero-resistance employees plan to embezzle from you even before you hire them, and as soon as they understand your systems well enough to see a pathway, they will start stealing. Since embezzlement is inevitable from this group, we want to screen these people out through a rigorous pre-employment screening process, which we will discuss in detail in Chapter 22.

High-resistance employees offer the lowest embezzlement risk because they require drastic circumstances to steal. The best strategy for managing risk with this group is to take an interest in the lives of your staff. The extreme circumstances needed to turn this cohort into thieves are things that you would likely be aware of if you knew your employees reasonably well. Identifying at-risk situations for this group allows for mitigation (for example, lending a financially desperate employee money instead of placing them in a position where they feel they have to steal it.)

Assuming that your pre-employment screening process is thorough, low-resistance employees are your biggest danger. Low-resistance employees represent a ticking time bomb. Sooner or later the right set of circumstances will exist for them to steal, and they will do so.

Measuring Resistance

How do we measure resistance and identify the low-resistance cohort? You may have already flagged the members of your team in this category, but here are a few strategies:

1. Examine past job-related behavior for ethical lapses, whether at your practice or in previous jobs. For a relatively recent hire, if you didn't contact previous employers to ask some questions, you might want to do so.

2. Consider the trend of previous changes in employment. "Lateral" employment moves (i.e., patterns of switching jobs without advancement or promotion) are always a red flag. Sometimes there is an identifiable reason for a lateral job move such as the new job being 10 miles closer to home or the employee's spouse being transferred to another city. If you cannot find a logical reason for job moves, this suggests some risk.

3. Thieves' personal lives can often offer clues. Gambling and alcohol or drug abuse are obvious risk factors but let's consider a few more. Many low-resistance employees exhibit a lot of instability in their personal lives. This may include relationship volatility with spouses or life partners or estrangement from family members. High-risk staff may move frequently or suffer foreclosures or serial bankruptcies. Interestingly, how they handle a motor vehicle can shed some light. A common factor we observe for many embezzlers is that they have many driving infractions on their records. It is typical to find eight, ten, or even 20 infractions including multiple speeding convictions, no seatbelt, expired registration, no insurance, etc. These infractions seemingly demonstrate a belief that the rules that govern everyone else do not apply to them. While based

on this comment it might be tempting to add motor vehicle abstracts to your pre-employment screening routine, **please** consult with your HR advisor before doing so. Unless the affected employee or applicant must drive for you as part of their duties, asking for this information that is not directly job-related may be prohibited where you live.

4. Test their honesty. This sounds inviting but needs to be done carefully. Some observers have advocated the doctor slipping an extra $20 into the practice's cash drawer to see whether the overage gets reported at the end of the day. If an integrity test is to be done, it probably needs to be considerably more controlled and sophisticated than the $20 experiment, and an expert should be consulted before any kind of "field test" is implemented.

This zero, low, and high resistance model provides an excellent framework for assessing and addressing the risk posed by individual employees.

3. A Deeper Understanding of Embezzlement

In Chapter 1, we learned that embezzlement is an abuse of a trust-based relationship. To decide if an action is embezzlement or something else, we need to develop our understanding of embezzlement more fully.

People sometimes use the words "embezzlement" and "fraud" interchangeably, but they do not mean the same thing.

Fraud is much broader than embezzlement and can be described as the use of deception for gain. For example, rolling back the odometer on a car you are selling to increase its value is fraud but not embezzlement. Embezzlement is a narrow subset of fraud.

While the specific laws that govern embezzlement, and the potential punishment, vary slightly across jurisdictions, the criminal act constituting embezzlement normally is required to contain the following four elements:

1. There must be a fiduciary relationship between the two parties; that is, there must be a reliance by one party on the other.
2. Property belonging to the victim must have become property of the embezzler or someone else at the direction of the perpetrator.
3. The perpetrator must have acquired the property through the relationship (rather than in some other manner).
4. The perpetrator's actions must have been intentional.

All four elements must be in place to have embezzlement. This requirement means that, for example, an employee who you accidentally overpay may have a requirement to repay the overcompensation but can't be described as having committed a criminal act because embezzlement requires intent on the part of the employee.

The practice owner's position is a bit murkier when a staff member defrauds an insurance company. While the required fiduciary relationship does not exist between your employee and the insurance company, when the practice owner is required to repay the insurance company for improperly received insurance benefits, this probably enters the domain of embezzlement.

Another form of fraud that we see sometimes involves a staff member conferring some kind of benefit on patients of the practice. Sometimes the recipients of this largesse are friends or family of the staff member (which we treat as embezzlement). In other cases, there is a *quid pro quo* given by the recipient to the employee for creating this benefit. We once saw a staff member receive a set of car tires from a patient in exchange for fraudulently arranging for some no-cost dentistry.

We also sometimes see a staff member confer benefits on people with whom the employee has no apparent connection. While there may be a connection that no one has discovered, at other times, this benevolence comes from a dislike of asking people for money or from resentment against someone whom the employee perceives to be a wealthy and greedy dentist.

Internally we refer to this kind of largesse as "Robin Hood" fraud (named after the fictional medieval character who stole from the rich to benefit the poor). Robin Hood fraud probably doesn't meet the definition of embezzlement. However, in most jurisdictions, it is still a crime and will be discussed more fully in Chapter 18.

Embezzlement Consists of Repeated Acts

One of the things that differentiates embezzlement from most other crimes is its repetitive nature. In contrast to many other types of stealing, an embezzler's goal is to victimize the same person repeatedly and do so without detection. Thus, embezzlement resembles a dripping faucet more than a burst pipe.

Embezzlement tends to start with small thefts, growing gradually over time as the embezzler refines his or her methodologies and determines how much can be stolen without attracting the practice owner's attention.

While there are outliers on both sides, our case files suggest that at the maturity of their schemes, many embezzlers exist in a bracket of stealing between 2% and 4% of a practice's collections. In a practice that brings in $750,000 per year, as a rough guide, we expect a thief's stealing to plateau at between about $15,000 and $30,000 per year, i.e., between $1,250 and $2,500 per month. Stealing this amount is normally effected through a series of small thefts that may occur more or less daily.

I'll discuss the financial implications of embezzlement more fully in Chapter 3, but for now, I simply want to give you a sense of embezzlement's gradual growth and nature of repetition.

3

How Big Is the Problem?

Embezzlement has been around since the beginning of recorded history. The Code of Hammurabi, the legal code of the Mesopotamians, is most famous for its "an eye for an eye" provision, but also specifically addressed embezzlement, as did the legal code for Ancient Egypt.[5]

The earliest record that I can find of embezzlement in a dental practice was in 1857 (which, by the way, also involved a murder).[6] When you consider that the world's first dental college, the Baltimore College of Dental Surgery, admitted its first class in 1840, it didn't take long for this problem to emerge.

[5]   B.P. Grenfell, A.S. Hunt, The Amherst Papyri, Being an Account of the Greek Papyri in the Collection of the Right Hon. Lord Amherst of Hackney, F.S.A. at Didlington Hall, Norfolk, I-II, 1900-1901)
[6]   Embezzlement in Dentistry is Not a Recent Phenomenon — This One From 1857 https://www.prosperident.com/embezzlement-in-dentistry-is-not-a-recent-phenomenon-this-one-from-1857/

Former Federal Reserve Chairman Alan Greenspan said this about embezzlement:

> "Corruption, embezzlement, fraud, these are all characteristics that exist everywhere. It is regrettably the way human nature functions, whether we like it or not... No one has ever eliminated any of that stuff."[7]

While measurement issues make the answer to the question of prevalence in dentistry somewhat elusive, a comparison of surveys taken of dentists over time shows that the problem is growing.

We briefly mentioned the 2019 CDP Survey performed by the American Dental Association's Center for Dental Practice. In this survey, 19,991 dentists were polled, and the astonishing result was that 48.64% of those who responded confirmed that they had been victims of embezzlement.[8]

It didn't stop there. As can be seen from the graph below, almost half of the dentists who reported being embezzled disclosed that they had been victims more than once, with 9% of respondents confirming that they had been victimized four or more times.

---

[7]   "Alan Greenspan Quote." A, www.azquotes.com/quote/1204472?ref= embezzlement.

[8]   American Dental Association. (2019). 2018 CDP Survey on Employee Theft in the Dental Practice. *Center for Dental Practice*

How Often Have You Been a Victim?

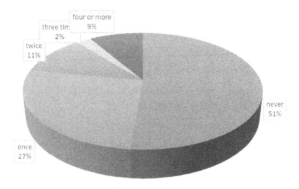

Figure 1 – Results of ADA 2019 Embezzlement Survey

If we simply multiply the number of dentists in each frequency category by the minimum frequency (i.e., 27% x 1, plus 11% x2 and so on), we can determine that, for every 100 dentists, there have already been at least 91 embezzlements that have taken place.

The percentage of dentists who report being embezzled is on the rise. In 2007, the ADA performed a similar survey, which found that 35% of the respondents had been victims[9], so in the 12 years between the two surveys, the percentage of dentists reporting embezzlement increased by more than a third (i.e.,

---

[9]   "Protecting Your Dental Office from Fraud & Embezzlement." American Dental Association. 2007. Accessed July 30, 2019. https://ebusiness.ada.org/assets/docs/2260.PDF?OrderID=227352.

13% of those surveyed). This growth is a significant and alarming trend.

Surveys on the prevalence of embezzlement in dentistry that have been done by other organizations, albeit less broadly based, have reported similar probabilities.

Statistics on embezzlement in dentistry and elsewhere suffer chronically from underreporting. Some dentists never realize that they have been stolen from, and others who know that they have been victims choose, for their own reasons, not to report their victimization. Accordingly, some of the 51% who reported no embezzlement in the ADA survey probably have been victims, but we cannot determine how many.

The other unknown is how many of those 51% will suffer embezzlement at some future date. It is certainly greater than zero, but also unquantifiable.

Moving from surveys taken across a large group of dentists to the relevance to an individual practice owner means translating these percentages into probabilities. Using the 2019 ADA survey as a baseline, if 49% of dentists have already been embezzled, what is the probability of the remaining 51% becoming victims in the remainder of their careers?

The math can be a bit daunting, but it's a pretty good bet that approximately half of those reporting that they had not yet been victimized will be stolen from at some future date. Add in some allowance for the non-detection and non-reporting of embezzlement, and it's a safe bet that 70% of dentists will be victims sooner or later.

With these probabilities being expressed on a "per dentist" basis, the risk faced by large multi-doctor practices and owners of multiple practices is even higher. I'll discuss the implications for these structures in Chapter 9.

Government, Charities, Healthcare

This high rate of victimization shouldn't come as a surprise – many studies suggest that healthcare entities are the third-most likely victimized entities for economic crime, behind charities and governments.[10]

There is a fundamental difference between these three types of entities and other commercial activities. Every business involves an exchange of money for goods or services of equal value. This exchange allows the possibility of measuring one side of the equation as a surrogate for the other. My former brother-in-law owns a chain of pizza restaurants, with several of them near university campuses. This is a situation where many transactions take place in cash, with a temptation to underreport income for tax purposes. When the tax authorities conducted an audit of one of his restaurants, the approach that they took was to contact his supplier of pizza boxes. From the number of boxes purchased by that restaurant, by applying an average cost per pizza they could approximate what the restaurant's revenue was. A significant difference between their calculation and the reported revenue would be suggestive of tax evasion.

---

[10]   Schnurer, Eric. "Just How Wrong Is Conventional Wisdom About Government Fraud?" The Atlantic. August 19, 2013. Accessed July 30, 2019. https://www.theatlantic.com/politics/archive/2013/08/everything-you-think-you-know-about-government-fraud-is-wrong/278690/.

By their nature, governments and charities do not lend themselves to that kind of analysis of their operations. Charities take money from one group and distribute it to another, and governments…well, they just take the money.

Healthcare entities do have monetary exchanges, but the exchange is imperfect compared with most other businesses. The cause of the imperfection is insurance, which, according to the National Association of Dental Plans, covers 77% of Americans.[11] Insurance can produce some level of indifference on the part of patients about the true cost of dental care. It can also provide many opportunities for an enterprising thief to steal.

How much money is stolen?

Sometimes embezzlement is minor, such as taking pens or toilet paper from your office. In other situations, it involves hundreds of thousands of dollars, or even a million or more dollars, taken over an extended period.

While it is sometimes tempting to dismiss low-value theft as more of an irritant than a real crime, the words of Professor Steve Albrecht should be kept in mind. Albrecht, who is a thought leader in the fraud investigation community, famously stated that "there are no small frauds; just large frauds that are caught early."[12] People who steal low-value items have already

---

[11]   Who has dental benefits today? The National Association of Dental Plans https://www.nadp.org/Dental_Benefits_Basics/Dental_BB_1.aspx
[12]   Albrecht, Steve, Ph.D., CFE, CPA. "Finishing Well by Starting Well." Accessed July 30, 2019. https://www.acfe.com/article.aspx?id=4294986390.

found a way to rationalize dishonesty, and we should expect that it is only a matter of time before they graduate to more significant theft.

As discussed in Chapter 2, we expect that, when their stealing matures, a typical embezzler will misappropriate between 2% and 4% of a practice's collections. They are normally able to continue doing this for some time. From a review of our case files, the average amount that a thief successfully steals from a dental practice before they get caught is $109,000,[13] making this problem far worse than an unremarkable nuisance.

While 2%-4% of collections seems like a modest number, the impact on a practice owner of this amount is proportionately much higher. Practice management guru Dr. Roger Levin stated in 2015 that the median overhead for a U.S. dental practice was 74.62%.[14] From the 25.38% remaining after overhead, the percentage stolen looms large indeed. An embezzler who steals 3% of collections is, therefore, gobbling up about 11% of a practice's profitability.

For many dentists, losing this amount to employee theft represents the difference between being able to save for retirement versus just having enough to pay their bills. Embezzlement can force an already struggling dentist over the edge and into bankruptcy.

The Association of Certified Fraud Examiners publishes an annual report on embezzlement called <u>Report to the Nations</u>.

---

[13]   Dunning, David G. *Dental Practice Transition: A Practical Guide to Management.* Wiley & Sons, Incorporated, John, 2016.

[14]   Levin, Roger P., *How does your overhead compare to national averages?* Dental Economics Aug 2015.

While its numbers reflect all data from all industries and are not specific to dentistry, in the 2018 edition, it pegged the median loss for occupational fraud in the United States at slightly over $100,000.[15] This broadly-based number does lend some support to Prosperident's internal data.

What Gets Stolen?

One of the differences between how embezzlement takes place in dentistry versus other businesses is that most dental embezzlement takes the form of diversion of incoming funds, which is often referred to as "skimming."

How a specific employee steals is a function of their access. Particularly in larger enterprises, relatively few people have access to incoming revenue, and typically embezzlement normally takes place by creating or increasing expenses. Consider, for example, how embezzlement might take place at a major airline. With most airline tickets purchased by credit card and airlines having eliminated the ability to pay with cash (or in some cases credit cards) for onboard purchases, relatively few airline employees can access incoming revenue.

Embezzlement by aircrew might involve fudging their expense reports or possibly stealing food or alcohol from flight catering. In the maintenance department, stealing might be people padding their hours or stealing and selling expensive tools or airplane parts.

---

[15]   "ACFE Report to the Nations: 2018 Global Fraud Study." ACFE. Accessed July 30, 2019. https://www.acfe.com/report-to-the-nations/2018/.

In contrast, in typical dental practices, all front-desk employees and office managers have access to incoming funds, which therefore represent a tempting target.

Expense-side stealing, such as pilfering supplies or tampering with payroll, certainly happens but with less frequency and fewer dollars stolen. In many cases, expense-side theft takes place because that is where the opportunity lies for a particular thief. For example, a bookkeeper may not have access to revenue or to practice management software but might be the person paying the bills. If this bookkeeper decides to steal, they will do so on the expense side because that is the only place they could steal. Clinical staff, without much access to incoming revenue, might sell stolen dental supplies online.

While the 2019 CDP Survey asked embezzlement victims what was stolen, 79% reported the theft of patient or insurance payments, and 40% reported the theft of services (e.g., free dentistry given to a thief's relatives) or theft of refunds due to patients. In contrast, only 48% reported payroll theft, and 38% reported the theft of consumables or resale products.[16]

Unfortunately, the ADA did not survey dollar losses from each theft type, but in our experience, larger dollar thefts invariably involve revenue theft.

The total responses to the ADA survey exceed 100% for two reasons. As discussed in Chapter 3, about half of the embezzlement victims had been stolen from more than once, and we know that most thieves combine multiple stealing

---

[16]   American Dental Association. (2019). 2018 CDP Survey on Employee Theft in the Dental Practice. *Center for Dental Practice*

methods. Like any prudent investor, thieves appreciate the value of diversification.

While cash and other monetary items are the biggest targets for dental practice embezzlement, my team also sees thefts of resale items like electric toothbrushes and whitening kits, consumables, and even thefts of dental equipment. Online marketplaces like eBay offer plenty of dental supplies and equipment for sale. Some of the equipment for sale is used or surplus gear that is no longer needed by a practice, but many of the items listed are new. While some of the new items listed for sale online are probably "gray market" merchandise that was diverted from somewhere along the supply chain, we have seen items being sold by a dental practice team member who deliberately over-ordered stock so that they could then sell it. While it is tempting for practice owners to grab some of the online "bargains" available, before you do, please give some thought to the probable origin of the item.

The Time Value of Money

One factor that is rarely mentioned in the literature is that the financial loss from embezzlement must be contextualized to the point in a dentist's career when it occurs.

If a dentist loses $100,000 to embezzlement immediately before her retirement, her retirement estate is diminished by $100,000.

But consider a new practice owner who is 30 years old and loses the same $100,000. Using a 7% growth rate, money doubles about every decade. Therefore, the $100,000 loss depletes his net worth by $200,000 at age 40, $400,000 at age 50, and so on. The amount foregone at age 65 using these parameters is just over a million dollars.

The long-term consequences of an early loss can be much higher, and early-career dentists can be particularly vulnerable to embezzlement.

I've heard the argument that "It's not such a big deal. The young dentist can work a bit harder, or spend a bit less, to make up this loss." Mathematically that is true -- increasing annual profitability by $7,720 for 35 years would replace the stolen funds, but I'm not sure it is relevant. Your ability to increase your annual take-home by $7,720 has nothing to do with whether you were embezzled or not. In other words, the young dentist in this situation could always be better off at retirement if not embezzled. The real question is what piece early career embezzlement will take from a dentist's retirement, and the answer is a lot of money.

The Emotional Impact of Embezzlement

As I mentioned in Chapter 1, monetary losses tell only part of the story. In contrast to much of the crime that we read about in the newspaper, embezzlement is a highly personal act. It is committed by someone known to, and trusted by, their victim. Therefore, the effect on the victim is entirely different from, for example, when some unknown person smashes your car window and steals your laptop. Many dentists who are victims struggle emotionally for years after the crime.

Embezzlement touches every corner of dentistry; it affects both general dentists and every dental specialty. Proprietorships, group practices, multi-office organizations, and large dental service organizations are all victimized. It takes place in urban practices and small-town offices. Some perpetrators are newly hired employees with "baggage" that was not identified, while others have worked in a practice for many years and have unblemished records when something causes them to start stealing.

There is a well-established correlation between the amount of time that someone has worked for an entity and the amount that they steal. In its 2018 Report to the Nations, the Association of Certified Fraud Examiners confirms the median loss when an employee had worked for an entity for less than a year to be $40,000. In contrast, the median loss when a thief had been with an organization for 6-10 years was $173,000.[17]

Practice owners are not the only victims when embezzlement happens in their practice. Embezzlement may affect other team members emotionally and financially. Associate dentists may have their compensation tampered with as part of an embezzlement scheme. It can affect the large community of people who sell products or offer consulting or other services to dentists when practice owners cannot upgrade their equipment or premises. Thus the losses are felt throughout the "dental economy."

---

[17]   "ACFE Report to the Nations: 2018 Global Fraud Study." ACFE. Accessed July 30, 2019. https://www.acfe.com/report-to-the-nations/2018/.

Last but not least, patients can also be victims of dental practice theft. First, some embezzlement patterns result in the practice management software carrying incorrect balances in patients' accounts. Certain embezzlement patterns may cause patients unwittingly to consume their annual or lifetime insurance limits while receiving no treatment in return. These things may cause a patient to lose confidence in their dentist.

A dentist's inability to keep up with technology and continuing education may mean that clinical care may suffer. Many post-embezzlement dentists find it challenging to be at their best emotionally when interacting with their patients.

Therefore, in addition to the obvious and devastating effect on the practice owner, embezzlement can impact many people in lesser ways.

4

Emotional Makeup of Embezzlers

One of the most frequent comments I hear, once the identity of an embezzler is confirmed, is that he or she is "the last person I could imagine stealing." The victim's surprise is understandable. We all have preconceptions about how criminals look, dress, speak, and act. Our mental image of what criminals look like is shaped by what we see on the news, popular T.V. dramas, and direct observations made in our communities.

Embezzlers very rarely fit the criminal stereotype we have created; many of them would remind you of Sunday school teachers (and some of them are!). The explanation of why embezzlers do not match our pre-formed picture of criminality is simple; You would never hire someone who looks like your imagined image of a thief. As an employer, you automatically eliminate certain people from your hiring process because they do not pass your personal "sniff test." However, your preconceived notion of what makes a person untrustworthy is probably narrow and unreliable.

Preconditions

The criminologist who probably had the most significant influence on developing our current understanding of economic crime was Donald Cressey. In his landmark 1973 book **Other People's Money**, Cressey proposed a framework called the Fraud Triangle. He theorized that there were three necessary preconditions for fraud; Pressure, Opportunity, and Rationalization.[18]

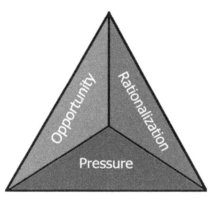

Figure 2 – Donald Cressey's Fraud Triangle

---

[18]   Cressey, Donald R. *Other People's Money; a Study in the Social Psychology of Embezzlement.* Montclair, NJ: Patterson Smith, 1973, page 30.

Pressure

Pressure can be either financial or emotional pressure, and I will often label the pressures that affect embezzlers as "Need" and "Greed."

Need

Needy embezzlers steal to address a financial need. Typically, some event has created an economic imbalance where the money leaving their household monthly exceeds their take-home pay. This deficiency threatens their ability to keep themselves afloat. The needy steal primarily to fund necessities like rent, utility, and mortgage payments. Many situations can propel a needy thief into action. A few common triggers are divorce, a spouse losing his or her job, being underprepared for retirement, or having an addiction of some kind.

Greedy Embezzlers

In his book The Great California Game, author Jonathan Gash said, "Fraud is the daughter of greed."[19] In contrast to the needy, greedy thieves steal to address an emotional deficit. In many cases, greedy thieves feel that society (represented by you, their employer) has failed to recognize the real value of their talents properly. These people steal to address this perceived inequity and tacitly prove how brilliant they are.

---

[19]   Gash, Jonathan. *The Great California Game*. Ulverscroft, 1991.

Greedy thieves may, perhaps even with justification, look at you as an intellectual peer. They conveniently forget the time, money, and commitment you made to become a dentist as well as the financial and emotional burdens of practice ownership.

The true profitability of your practice is irrelevant. Most members of your team, including any embezzlers you might be harboring, chronically overestimate what you take home. This overestimation fuels the embezzler's perception of income inequity. In a greedy thief's simplified worldview, it seems unfair that you earn many times what they do when the value of their contribution approaches yours.

Greedy thieves may also derive emotional pleasure from the act of successfully taking a risk; they are somewhat analogous to the celebrity shoplifters we occasionally hear about in the news. CPA and fraud investigator Bill Barrett once described white-collar criminals like this:

> Committing crimes does give its perpetrators a thrill. High-dollar criminals describe their machinations as having a "kick." They feel as if they're playing a game, and it's the game of their lives. Behaviorists agree. Money is a "generalized reinforcer," linked with many positive factors directly, and often taking on a symbolic power of its own, yielding a condition of strength.[20]

---

[20]   Barrett, Bill. *Inside the Mind of the White-Collar Criminal*. https://www. accountingweb.com/technology/trends/inside-the-mind-of-the-white-collar-criminal, August 2013.

A spectacular example of this took place in an investigation that my team carried out. The embezzler had been stealing from her doctor for several years when luck shone upon her; she won a $3 million prize in the State Lottery. Most dental team members having had that kind of windfall would quickly quit their jobs, and as a parting act would feel empowered to tell their doctor whatever they had always wanted to say but did not feel empowered to do so until now.

Not only this embezzler did not resign but she also continued stealing. But here is the interesting part: after her big lottery win, the amount she was taking monthly from her doctor actually increased. Since she demonstrably did not need the stolen money, we can only conclude that her stealing was because she continued to crave the kick described by Bill Barrett.

One of the differentiating characteristics of greedy thieves is how they spend their money. Needy thieves steal to protect their basic standard of living, and money goes to groceries, rent, car payments, and other necessities. In contrast, greedy thieves tend to spend their ill-gotten gains conspicuously and often on luxury items that would otherwise be unaffordable. We have seen thieves purchase $140,000 automobiles, yachts, and $8,000 front-row concert tickets. In one notable instance, we saw an embezzler who had chartered a plane to take her friends on a shopping trip. The "egotistic" spending that my team often encounters when investigating reinforces my view that greedy thieves are stealing to address deficits in self-esteem.

Opportunity

The next precondition for embezzlement is opportunity, and unfortunately, opportunities exist in every practice.

The biggest misconception, and a major enabling factor for embezzlement, is the belief that policies, procedures, and a system of "checks and balances" can prevent theft. This common misunderstanding affects not only practicing dentists but also many in the sizeable consulting community that provides business advice to dentists.

The reason for the misconception is an honest one. Most of us understand other types of crime better than embezzlement, which creates a tendency for us to assume that what works in controlling other kinds of criminal activity will also prevent embezzlement.

Most people realize that an alarm system installed in a house or business dramatically reduces the chance of burglary. A 2012 University of North Carolina Charlotte report concluded that 60% of burglars would not rob houses with alarm systems.[21] Similarly, locking your car's doors decreases the probability of your car's contents being stolen by a factor of 270%.[22] People assume that the same approach, i.e., increasing the perceived

---

[21] Kuhns, Joseph. *Understanding Decisions to Burglarize from the Offender's Perspective.* University of North Carolina at Charlotte, 2015. doi:10.13140/2.1.2664.4168.

[22] Farrell, Graham, Andromachi Tseloni, and Nick Tilley. "The Effectiveness of Vehicle Security Devices and Their Role in the Crime Drop." *Criminology & Criminal Justice* 11, no. 1 (2011): 21–35. https://doi.org/10.1177/1748895810392190.

difficulty of stealing, or will reduce the likelihood of being embezzled, and that is where the analogy gets misapplied.

The difference between burglary and embezzlement is simple; Burglars can switch victims far more easily than embezzlers. When a burglar standing on your doorstep spots an alarm company sticker on your door or hears a Doberman barking inside, they reconsider their plan. Reconsideration is easy; they simply shift their focus from your house to whichever of your neighbors they consider to be the least protected. From your narrow personal perspective, your protective measures were effective because they protected your house from crime. However, your control measures did not convert a would-be thief into a law-abiding citizen; they merely forced an adaptation to an easier nearby target.

Here is where analogizing embezzlement to burglary reaches its limit. For a burglar, changing victims is a natural and easy adaptation. It involves walking a few steps down the street and finding a less-protected target.

In contrast, changing victims is a significant undertaking for an embezzler. It involves them quitting their job and finding a new one, preferably with a doctor whom they have assessed and determined to be an easier target. They then need to spend enough time in their new practice to understand the controls and systems and gain their new doctor's trust. Then, if all goes according to plan, they can begin stealing. At a minimum, this would take several months. Most thieves are not that patient, and a much easier adaptation is to keep working for you, observing you, and finding a different way to steal from you.

What embezzlers can control, and therefore, what you can influence, is not their choice of their victim (spoiler alert: their victim will always be you!); it is their choice of methodology. If you can block an embezzler's first idea for stealing from you, they will neither abandon their plan to embezzle nor choose an alternative victim. Instead, they will stick with you and quickly move on to their second, third, or twelfth possible methodology until they find something that works. Moreover, with dental offices being highly porous in this respect, thieves have many options. Most thieves will employ multiple methods of stealing simultaneously (the norm is three concurrent methods). They will often discard some of their methodologies over time and replace them with new ones. In some cases, this is done to make detection more difficult, and in others, as thieves gain experience with stealing, they can refine their tradecraft.

When relating this information to Cressey's Fraud Triangle, the opportunity should be viewed as a binary factor because from the perspective of an embezzler, as we discussed in Chapter 2, opportunity either exists or does not. For embezzlement, more opportunity does not correlate with the increased probability of theft. Similarly, reducing, but not eliminating, opportunity does not decrease the likelihood. Assume that you have a motivated thief in your office - one who has studied you carefully. What is the chance that they will be able to find some method of going through or around your controls? Sadly, the probability is excellent.

Rationalization

Rationalization is normally the final stop in someone's journey to becoming an embezzler. We all learned when we were toddlers that it was wrong to take other people's things.

In an article in that spellbinding publication for accountants, *CPA Journal*, authors Natalia Mintchik, Ph.D., CPA, and Jennifer Riley, Ph.D., CPA state the following:

> "To be able to commit fraud, ordinary people need to rationalize to quiet the morality-based inner protests that would otherwise preclude them from engaging in such behavior."[23]

Rationalization is the ability of someone to set aside the deeply ingrained understanding that stealing is wrong.

When I talked about "Resistance" in Chapter 2, I discussed the propensity of someone to break the rules when under a certain amount of pressure. One way to visualize rationalization is an ethical "bar" that a thief must be able to jump over before stealing. This bar has different heights for different people, and a variety of factors can contribute to enabling a thief to lower the bar and thus rationalize stealing more easily. Another way

---

[23] Mintchik, Natalia, and Jennifer Riley. "Rationalizing Fraud." The CPA Journal, April 9, 2019. https://www.cpajournal.com/2019/04/15/rationalizing-fraud/.

of expressing resistance is how low that ethical bar is for a given person or how easily it can be lowered situationally.

Sometimes, the inadvertent actions of a dentist may have the effect of lowering the bar for someone in their office. Suppose team members watch you cutting ethical corners, possibly cheating on your income taxes, or doing something that staff members interpret as rubbing your relative affluence in their faces. These actions make it much easier for them to justify stealing from you.

I remember a case where a doctor had taken his entire team to a conference in an exotic location. The goodwill that he intended to generate for his team with this perk was undone when everyone got to the airport and realized that the doctor had purchased first-class tickets for himself and his wife while consigning the rest of the team to squeeze into coach seats on the same plane.

Another doctor I know used to complain regularly to his team about the high cost of repairs for his high-end Mercedes. It does not require much imagination to understand the animosity this caused, especially since he was clumsily letting his team know that his car cost more than any of them made annually by working for him.

At a minimum, this kind of behavior, intentional or not, shows the doctor to be insensitive. The other interpretation of these types of actions to a would-be embezzler is you are handing them the moral justification to steal.

Some of the rationalizations that we encounter regularly include:

- I am only borrowing the money and plan to repay it. If there is an intent to repay in the mind of the embezzler, then it is not really stealing, is it? Many embezzlers start with this view, but as their embezzlement continues over time and the amount stolen grows; eventually, many discard this rationalization.
- The practice owes me the money. This rationalization can come from a very narrow perspective (for example, that the thief is working hours beyond what he or she is getting paid) or from a more generalized perception that the wealthy dentist exploits the thief by under compensating him or her. Criminologists refer to this as a **claim of entitlement**.
- I am largely responsible for the practice's success. Some thieves will go as far as to construct an otherwise unrecognized partnership in their mind between the practice owner and them. This rationalization is particularly easy when the doctor is clinically focused and appears to have no interest in or understanding of the practice's business functioning.
- I make far more money for the practice than I steal. Literature refers to this rationalization as the **Metaphor of the Ledger**, where a thief compares the good work they believe they do against the amount they steal.
- The practice deserves to be stolen from. This notion that the practice owner is getting the justice they deserve often comes from believing that the owner is exploiting the patients or other third parties, such

as insurance companies. This rationalization is called **condemning the condemners.**

- I only took a little bit, and the practice owner will not miss it. This logic is the **denial of injury** rationalization.
- Others are doing it too. Criminologists call this a **claim of relative acceptability/normality.**
- The Doctor told me to do it. This reasoning is sometimes called the **denial of responsibility** rationalization.
- It was out of my control. This embezzler claims that economic forces or other outside events "forced" them to do it. This rationalization is also a **denial of responsibility.**[24]

Embezzlers may use one or several of these rationalizations to convince themselves that their stealing was justified.

Profiles of Embezzlers

What are the personality traits of an embezzler? People who embezzle can display a wide variety of behaviors, which makes profiling them a bit of a challenge. Like every private investigator, I consider myself an armchair psychologist. Here are some of the more common profiles I see.

---

[24] For this discussion, labeling of rationalizations is largely based on a framework proposed in Haugh, Todd, *White Collar Rationalizations,* Business Law Prof Blog, May 2015, https://lawprofessors.typepad.com/business_law/2015/05/white-collar-rationalizations.html

The Narcissistic Sociopath

Many Greedy thieves display both sociopathic characteristics and the markers of narcissism. Psychological literature recognizes this combination as a narcissistic sociopath.[25]

Population studies suggest that about 6% of the population have narcissistic personality disorder, and 4% have Anti-Social Personality Disorder, more commonly referred to as sociopathy.[26] A significant portion of each of these cohorts also belongs to the other; literature suggests that between one and two percent of the population exhibit both characteristics of narcissism and sociopathy.[27]

The accepted traits of an antisocial personality disorder include:

1. Superficial charm and intelligence.
2. Unreliability.
3. Untruthfulness.
4. Lack of remorse.
5. Inadequately motivated antisocial behavior.
6. Delusions of invincibility.

---

[25] Stein, D. (2016, August 11). Narcissist or Sociopath? Similarities, Differences and Signs. https://www.psychologytoday.com/us/blog/the-integrationist/201608/narcissist-or-sociopath-similarities-differences-and-signs retrieved August 15, 2020
[26] Eddy, Bill LCSW, JD, Are Narcissists and Sociopaths Increasing?, Psychology Today, April 2018
[27] Lents, Nathan H., Ph.D., The Evolutionary Role of Narcissistic Sociopaths, Psychology Today, December 2018

7. Failure to learn by experience.
8. Failure to follow any life plan.[28]

Some behavioral characteristics of narcissism are:

1. Self-importance. In dentistry, they often think they should be your "partner" and may even refer to the patients as "their" patients.
2. Focus on appearance.
3. Exaggerate achievements and abilities.
4. Believe they are of special or high status.
5. Think they can only be understood by similar people.
6. Need for admiration.
7. Sense of entitlement and expect favorable treatment.
8. Lack of empathy.
9. Envious of others or thinks others envy them.[29]

Many of the embezzlers I have encountered, particularly the "serial embezzlers" who have stolen from more than a single practice, fit the narcissistic sociopath category closely.

Although you will not find these in scholarly publications, some other profiles that we have seen embezzlers frequently fit we describe as the Hero, the Control Freak, and the Sugar Momma.

---

[28]   *Diagnostic and Statistical Manual of Mental Disorders DSM-5.* Arlington, VA: American Psychiatric Association, 2013.

[29]   *Diagnostic and Statistical Manual of Mental Disorders DSM-IV.* Arlington, VA: American Psychiatric Association, 1994.

The Hero

The Hero looks for a practice that is really struggling. This practice is often a disorganized office with many unpaid insurance claims and accounts receivable that are out of control. The Hero claims that they have cleaned up bigger messes before and that they love a challenge. They know too well that you will be feeling so relieved at having found the perfect person to take on the herculean task of getting your office back on track that the last thing that will occur to you is to call that last office that the Hero supposedly whipped into shape to obtain a job reference. While the Hero can sometimes achieve some short-term success with these problems, they have considerably oversold their experience and abilities. Their true focus is cleaning you **out,** not up.

The Control Freak

I'm sure that you can conjure up a mental picture of the Control Freak. He or she is the person of whom the other staff is terrified. He or she guards their duties jealously and reacts aggressively to anything they perceive as an encroachment. This territoriality will often extend to their workspace and "their" computer, and another team member who sits at their desk or touches this person's computer without the Control Freak's permission will likely receive a dose of wrath. The Control Freak may combine their tyranny over staff with subservience to you (which one of my team labels the "Teacher's Pet"). Control Freaks may do things like locking the door to their office when they go to lunch and will never cross-train any team members on their job, even if they have told you that they must. Control Freaks seldom take a vacation and are never sick. This person may work extra hours, often arriving before everyone else or staying behind after work to "finish up."

For a dentist who enjoys the clinical part of their practice and despises running the business, the Control Freak presents as the answer to their prayers; this is someone who will free the doctor to do dentistry and will take care of everything else.

The Sugar Momma

At the opposite end of the behavioral spectrum is the Sugar Momma (who, of course, can be of any gender). The Sugar Momma is the person who bestows largesse on other team members. Sometimes it is baking cookies and bringing them into the office for the team; at other times, it is tampering with the pay of one or more employees to pay them for hours beyond what they worked or giving them a pay raise that wasn't approved by you.

Why do they do this? You may have heard the saying actions "You don't look a gift horse in the bicuspids." Over time, the Sugar Momma's actions cause the loyalty of staff members to be redirected to the Sugar Momma. This loyalty means that, for example, if these staff members have a concern about something going on at the office, they are far more likely to go to Sugar Momma than to you with that concern, allowing Sugar Momma the chance to assuage whatever the concern is.

This relationship does not mean that Sugar Momma's chosen ones are complicit in his or her illicit activities. However, because Sugar Momma has "intercepted" the loyalty that should be directed at you, he or she can dramatically reduce the risk of being outed by a whistleblower.

And this hijacking of loyalty may not be limited to staff. We see with many embezzlers that, over time, they gradually cause a turnover of the external people who provide goods and services to their own "team". They may prompt a change in the IT person, the primary dental supplier, and even the accountant to someone with whom Sugar Momma already has a relationship. This change will be made under the guise of obtaining better prices or better service and will be misinterpreted by you as Sugar Momma looking out for your interest. However, the result is that the external advisors to the practice, who are sometimes in a position to realize that something is "off," have stronger loyalty to Sugar Momma than you. Since these people now receive part of their income due to having been selected by Sugar Momma, they will accord Sugar Momma the benefit of the doubt in any ambiguous situation. If they do develop concerns, they will bring them to Sugar Momma rather than you.

The Irony of these Personality Traits

One of the interesting manifestations of these profiles is that they each display some characteristics of what many dentists view as ideal employees. Clearly, the Hero can identify an office where the dentist is drowning and desperately wants a savior. The Control Freak looks like a hyper-dedicated employee, and many doctors love the idea of having that "take charge" person as office manager and being able to withdraw mentally from the minutiae of administering their practice. The Control Freak offers the promise of that. I'll discuss the dangers of the dentist disengaging from the practice's non-clinical elements in Chapter 30. The Sugar Momma is popular with staff (and often patients), and this person is rarely the practice's nexus of interpersonal drama.

How Does the Economy Factor In?

I am often asked whether more embezzlement occurs when the economy is booming or in recession. There have been relatively few scholarly studies on this issue, and those that have been done suggest that the effect of economic conditions on the overall level of embezzlement is small.[30]

My experience is that, while the total amount embezzled doesn't change much across different parts of the business cycle, economic conditions affect our two dental embezzlement cohorts differently. Tough times create more situations of financial desperation, and therefore, more needy thieves. We saw this clearly during and after the financial crisis of 2007-2008.

Arguably the most famous economist of the 20th Century, John Kenneth Galbraith, said this about an earlier economic event, the Great Depression of 1929, when he wrote, "In many

---

[30] Geppert, June Panter Relationship of embezzlement and the economic condition in the United States economy, PhD Dissertation, Capella University, May 2016

ways, the effect of the crash on embezzlement was more significant than on suicide."[31]

When the economy is doing well, fewer people are living close to the financial brink. However, what we notice is that a robust economy brings out the greedy thieves. When working in a dental office, these people are paid hourly or on a salary. They see themselves falling behind their friends who are entrepreneurs or investors, and it bothers them to see others getting ahead more quickly than they are.

What is not often understood by dentists is how powerful the motivation is to steal and how the combination of determination, cleverness, and knowledge of how your office operates creates a perfect storm for embezzlement to be successfully carried out, at least for a time.

What Job Do They Have in the Practice?

The 2019 CDP Survey asked respondents which position in their office the thief occupied. Of those who gave a specific response, 70.8% of stealing was from someone in an administrative position, with the other 29.2% coming from someone occupying a clinical role.

People in supervisory positions were the most likely to steal, accounting for 35.9% of the responses, with lower-level administrative positions like administrative assistant, treatment

---

[31]   Shaughnessy, Don. "In Economics, What Is 'The Bezzle?'" *MoneyFYI*, 14 Nov. 2013, moneyfyi.wordpress.com/2013/11/15/5358/.

coordinator, and financial coordinator accounting for 32.4%. Bookkeepers were responsible 2.5% of the time.[32]

Will a Thief Stop Stealing?

In a 2019 presentation at a conference of the Association of Certified Fraud Examiners, John Hurlimann CFE, the director of Internal Audit investigations for computer hardware manufacturer Intel, said the following three things about embezzlers:

1. They cannot stop. The only time they stop is when they get caught or leave the business for greener pastures.
2. The amount stolen increases over time.
3. Others have noticed something is not right.[33]

Mr. Hurlimann's observations are completely consistent with Prosperident's experience. I have never seen a thief stealing from a practice who stopped embezzling while continuing to work at the practice. Normally the only thing that stops them is something structural such as being fired or moving away because their spouse gets transferred.

The initial behavior of embezzlers reminds me of watching fish near my bait when fishing in my teens. I grew up within walking distance of the ocean and spent considerable time

[32]   American Dental Association. (2019). 2018 CDP Survey on Employee Theft in the Dental Practice. *Center for Dental Practice*

[33]   Hurlimann, John. *Mastering Emerging Fraud Detection Tools and Techniques*. Proceedings of ACFE Global Fraud Conference, Austin, TX. June 2019.

fishing. A fish would normally take an experimental nibble or two (which excitingly caused the red and white bobber that I used for suspending the bait to bounce around) before the fish went wholeheartedly after the bait and became my family's dinner. Like what those fish did, it is normal to see a couple of experimental "nibbles," which may even be prompted by some accidental occurrence that results in money left over after a patient's account balance has been paid.

Often after the first couple of tentative forays into stealing, there is a pause, which may last a month or so, before a thief recommences in earnest. I guess that the purpose of this waiting period is to see whether the theft gets noticed by someone while there is still the ability to explain it away as a simple error. When the thief realizes that no one has noticed, they return to stealing and in a more aggressive way. Unlike fishing, there is no equivalent of a bobber to alert you to the activity around your practice's money and no hook and fishing line embedded in the thief.

Will other employees report fraud?

Many airports have signs that read "If you see something, say something." We all accept that the vigilance of travelers has a role to play in keeping airports and airplanes safe. The role of other employees in keeping a dental practice safe from an embezzler is less well-developed.

Most large corporations have anonymous "tip lines" where someone can report the actions of a co-worker. In big companies, whistleblowers are the single biggest source of the discovery of embezzlement. Information from the Association of Certified Fraud Examiners covering all businesses shows that tips from co-workers uncover more than 40% of embezzlement in the broader business community.[34]

However, co-workers reporting embezzlement is less frequent in dentistry. According to the 2007 ADA survey of dental embezzlement victims that I mentioned in Chapter 2, whistleblowers accounted for only 9.3% of embezzlement discovery in dental practices, so dental employees report on their co-workers far less often than people in other businesses do.

This abnormally low incidence of embezzlement being outed by a whistleblower in dental practices is easily explainable. No employee wants to be branded as a "rat" or a "snitch." Because most dental practices have few employees, and even fewer involved in administration, it is natural for an employee who is thinking about coming forward to fear for their anonymity. When a whistleblower does approach the practice owner, even if that owner tries to keep their identity secret, the list of possible whistleblower candidates is extremely short, and it is normally quite easy for a thief to identify who flagged them. The perceived lack of anonymity for whistleblowers is enough to keep many employees from coming forward to the owner of the practice.

In those infrequent cases where a concerned staff member does approach you, they are often a new team member who does not have a strong bond with the embezzler and thus chooses to approach the practice owner rather than the embezzler.

---

[34]   "ACFE Report to the Nations: 2018 Global Fraud Study." ACFE. Accessed July 30, 2019. https://www.acfe.com/report-to-the-nations/2018/.

In cases where embezzlement was discovered in some other way, post-mortem interviews we have done with uninvolved staff in practices that were embezzled reveal that typically one or more staff members knew that something was not right but simply didn't feel comfortable bringing a hunch to the practice owner. What I think many did not say is that they were unwilling to "rat" on a colleague when they were less than certain, so they chose to remain silent. If this discomfort can be addressed, the potential to stop embezzlement more quickly clearly exists.

Accordingly, we should not count on other employees to realize that embezzlement is taking place or bring suspicious actions to the practice owner's attention. If an employee does feel sufficiently concerned to approach you, please be appreciative of the risk that they have taken in coming to you, assure them that you will have their concerns investigated, and then follow through on your promise. It's difficult to "snitch" on a co-worker, so please be appreciative and respectful of someone who values you enough to bring his or her concerns to you.

Encouraging Team Members to Come Forward

What can be done to facilitate a staff member who has concerns to approach the practice owner? There are a few things that you can do to help capture this significant opportunity.

- Have a whistleblower policy in place. As discussed, someone planning to discuss concerns about a co-worker or superior to you faces considerable uncertainty. You can reduce that uncertainty dramatically by having a clear set of principles about how you will handle whistleblower events. Since you have no way of knowing when an employee is trying to decide whether to approach you, these principles need to be communicated in advance, and having a protective policy as part of your employee manual is probably the best way to do this.

- Reward whistleblowers. We talked about misdirected loyalty earlier in this chapter. One of the best ways to redirect that loyalty back to you is to offer rewards to whistleblowers whose information saves you money.
- Talk the talk, then walk the walk. If you promise something in the policy, deliver on it, even if doing so is inconvenient. If you fail at this, your employees will never trust you again.

If your employee manual does not already contain protective provisions for whistleblowers, we have a well-written draft policy that I am happy to share. Email us at requests@prosperident.com and we will be glad to send it to you.

What if an Outside Advisor Expresses Concern?

Sometimes an outside advisor who could be a practice management consultant, bookkeeper, software trainer, I.T. person, accountant, dental supply representative, practice broker if you are selling your practice, or someone else, may approach you with concerns about your practice.

If this happens, please do a few things:

1. Take them seriously. These advisors typically deal with many different practices and have a good frame of reference for deciding that something is not right with yours. No matter what level of disbelief you have, consider the possibility that they see something that you have overlooked.

2. Appreciate the risk that they took in approaching you. Most of these people are compensated based on how much work they do for you or how much of their product you buy. It would often be easier to keep their mouths shut and ignore whatever gives them concern, and they have chosen to take a more difficult and riskier path by approaching you with their concerns. Raising this issue may pit them against a long-term, trusted employee of yours. You should appreciate this and say so.

3. Don't shoot the messenger. Even if you are convinced that they are dead wrong, don't punish someone commercially who approaches you on this basis. Retaliating against the messenger will cause the word to spread in the local dental community and make everyone skittish about giving you honest advice.

When either an employee or an outside advisor expresses concern about embezzlement in your practice, you should also be concerned.

5

"I Live in A Small Town" and Other Myths of Immunity

I am not referring to the catchy John Mellencamp tune of 1985, but instead, I am pointing out one of the many fallacies to which dentists subscribe while convincing themselves that they are "immune" from embezzlement.

We all want to believe that our team members are honest and that they would never steal from us, and most of the time, this is true.

However, a significant portion of the population will commit dishonest acts under the right circumstances. A shocking statistic is that 75% of employees report having stolen from their employer.[35] When you combine the size of this cohort with the

---

[35] Employee theft: Why do employees steal? California Restaurant Association. (2017, May 1). https://www.calrest.org/labor-employment/employee-theft-why-do-employees-steal

considerable number of team members that the typical dentist turns over in his or her career, the result is that at least four in five dentists eventually become victims of embezzlement.

The biggest mistake overly trusting dentists make is underestimating the ingenuity and determination of those who embezzle. They latch onto certain fallacies that they believe provide them with immunity. Life is more comfortable when you can convince yourself that you are safe from the world's terrible problems, so naturally, humans are receptive to the concept that our situation somehow protects us from the transgressions of others.

One of the best statements about susceptibility to embezzlement comes from Certified Fraud Examiner Donn LeVie Jr., who said: "If you do not think you are at risk of becoming a fraud victim, then you're likely at risk of becoming a fraud victim."[36]

When I speak to live audiences, I get asked a lot of "probability" questions. Understandably, people want to know whether embezzlement is more likely at an early stage of their career or later, whether orthodontists are more likely than periodontists to be victims, or whether U.S. dentists are victimized more often than Canadian dentists.

While this answer often doesn't sit well with those asking the questions, every practicing dentist faces that 70% lifetime probability that I mentioned.

---

[36]   LeVie, Donn, Jr. "Who's More Susceptible to Fraud?" Fraud Magazine. January/February 2019. Accessed July 30, 2019. https://www.fraud-magazine.com/article.aspx?id=4295004205.

Is Embezzlement a Crime of Opportunity?

While the perpetrators have some definable characteristics, the victims have almost none. Contrary to what many observers have written, embezzlement is **not** a crime of opportunity.

A good definition of a crime of opportunity is:

> "A crime that is committed without planning, when the perpetrator sees that they have the chance to commit the act at that moment and seizes it. Such acts have little or no premeditation."[37]

Because embezzlement is normally a series of repeated thefts, this definition effectively excludes embezzlement. Even if the first theft in a series was committed on an impulse, the inevitable repetitions are carefully planned and implemented, with the thief taking full advantage of their knowledge of the practice's systems and the owner's habits to steal undetected.

Because embezzlement is a premeditated, as opposed to opportunistic, crime, the victim's circumstances have no real impact on the probability. A team member's decision to become dishonest has relatively little to do with you, and it is far more likely to be a manifestation of their own needs and wants. If we are dealing with an employee with low resistance as we defined it in Chapter 2, it doesn't take much for these employees

---

[37] "Crime of Opportunity." Wikipedia. Wikimedia Foundation, November 17, 2019. https://en.wikipedia.org/wiki/Crime_of_opportunity.

to start embezzling. For employees with higher resistance, stealing might still happen when the right set of circumstances coalesces. So as a practice owner, the risk you face could be expressed as the probability that you hire a low-resistance employee, plus the probability that a high-resistance employee faces an extreme situation.

If embezzlement were a crime of opportunity, then logically, a practice with less opportunity should be less likely to be embezzled. To extend this logic further, if this were true, reducing opportunity in a practice would also reduce the chances that the practice would be embezzled. As we discussed in Chapter 4, this does not pan out in practice.

Checks and Balances

Many dentists, accountants, and practice management consultants refer to the concept of "checks and balances" as the antidote for embezzlement. In my experience, this phrase is often thrown around by people who have, at best, a superficial understanding of what it means in a dental practice.

Back in the days when I used to work in a bank, many activities required the involvement of two or even three people. The vaults that were in each branch had two combination locks. Even something basic like when a customer needed a bank draft required a teller to prepare a requisition, and then two "officers" to sign the draft. Banks can do this because they are large, well-staffed, and reasonably profitable organizations.

In comparison, many dental practices are administered by a single person. In a larger practice, it is possible to involve multiple employees in certain activities, but doing so always comes at a cost to productivity.

Furthermore, the employee who is most likely stealing from you often plays a crucial role in whatever checking and balancing is done, which normally allows them to skirt around the systems that you have in place in your office to deter theft.

There are strategies for dividing duties between you and your team that can lessen your embezzlement risk dramatically. We will discuss those strategies in detail in Chapter 20.

Are Younger or Older Dentists More Vulnerable?

While there is no correlation between the likelihood of embezzlement and your career stage, it is my view, based on more than thirty years as an investigator, that dentists who are in the first five or the last five years of their careers are more likely to take longer to realize that they have a problem than mid-career dentists. In the case of new dentists, a combination of their inexperience in business and the burden of juggling their new practices with the effort needed to build their clinical skills and raise young families all at the same time can hinder their opportunities to recognize the early stages of embezzlement. (We discussed the financial impact of the time value of money on early-career dentist victims in Chapter 3.)

Dentists who are in the twilight years of their careers are, hopefully, financially secure, and often do not feel the need to watch their pennies as closely as they once did. These seasoned practitioners are more likely to have had the same team members for years, and understandably they may feel a level of trust for their experienced front office staff. One could also assume that many senior dentists, who started practicing before practices were computerized, have never become fully conversant with their practice management software. Unfortunately, this puts them at a marked disadvantage when it comes to early detection of embezzlement.

Some dentists believe that embezzlement is an urban problem and that dentists who practice in cities, especially large cities, face higher embezzlement risk because they frequently hire people they do not know. It is a misconception that, because those employed by a small-town dentist are generally well-known to the dentist, and frequently are current or former patients, this will insulate the dentist from being victimized; we have ample case files that demonstrate otherwise.

Over the years, we have encountered many dental specialists who believe embezzlement is primarily a problem for general dentists. Other doctors were convinced that by paying their team members a premium above the norm for their area, they could purchase their team members' honesty. Some are convinced that by carefully checking the day-end report from their practice management software, they can make themselves embezzlement-proof.

While all these actions have good intentions as methods for preventing theft, none of them make much difference when we profile how or why someone steals. This will be discussed in Chapter 12.

The fact that a staff member is actively involved in organized religion will not protect the practice owner. We have heard many victims disbelievingly say, "But she goes to my church."

A Selfish Crime

Embezzlement happens for one simple reason: someone who works for you decides that they are entitled to your money. As discussed in Chapter 4, the factors that push a team member towards a decision to steal from you have a lot to do with them and very little to do with you. When the necessary elements exist, people embezzle, which can happen in any practice, anywhere, and at any time. No practice is immune. As for the profiling of thieves, while there are some psychographic and behavioral markers, which I also discussed in Chapter 4, demographic profiling is challenging. Thieves can be in their 20s or 70s of any ethnic or religious background, be urban or rural, work in large or small practices, and have any level of education and experience.

The Perception of Detection

Scholarly publications consistently suggest that increasing the perception that embezzlement will be detected or increasing the perceived punishment, decreases the likelihood that embezzlement will occur.[38]

While this hypothesis has considerable intuitive appeal, there is very little evidence-based research supporting it. By its nature, perception of detection is difficult to study in the "real world," and the published empirical work is limited to

---

[38] See, for example, Richard C. Hollinger and John P. Clark, Deterrence in the Workplace: Perceived Certainty, Perceived Severity, and Employee Theft, Social Forces, Volume 62, Issue 2, December 1983

experiments where people play games in laboratory settings. This type of experimentation cannot replicate the raw emotion that exists when someone is one missed mortgage payment away from having their house foreclosed. My experience suggests that this factor is not as influential as many believe.

Do Men Embezzle?

When speaking to dental audiences, I sometimes get asked this question by an audience member. If you look at the Hall of Shame part of our website, it is evident that the overwhelming majority of embezzlers (<95%) in dental practices are female. This dominance is not necessarily because one gender is more prone to stealing than the other. While dentistry itself has achieved approximate gender parity, the same cannot be said for people in administrative roles in dentistry (or, for that matter, dental assistants and dental hygienists); the majority of people filling each of these professions are female.

Because administrative positions in dentistry are not regulated occupations, gender statistics for them are not available. However, in dental assisting, which is probably a reasonable surrogate, especially given that many people who start as dental assistants move on to front-desk and office management positions, 94% of registered dental assistants in the US are female.[39]

So it isn't that men don't steal, but their numbers in dental practice administration are so small that it is easy to conclude otherwise.

---

[39]   https://datausa.io/profile/soc/dental-assistants#demographics

A former Prosperident team member, Kelly Paxton CFE, has achieved international renown for her study and knowledge of what she labels "pink collar crime," by which she means embezzlement by lower-level employees (as opposed to white-collar crime, typically conducted by higher-level employees in large enterprises.) Kelly suggests that men are responsible for stealing larger amounts of money (median = $156,000) compared to women (median = $89,000).[40] Female offenders tend to commit embezzlement with a higher probability but steal less money. Kelly also suggests that women invoke different rationalizations for their actions than men do.

Serial Embezzlers

The dental profession has its fair share of "serial embezzlers" who victimize more than one office. When they get caught and fired for stealing from a practice, these thieves move to another office and resume stealing, often within weeks. Strategies for avoiding hiring one of these ticking time bombs are detailed in Chapter 22. To read about a truly prolific serial embezzler, I encourage you to read an article called Steals then Squeals I wrote several years ago detailing some interviews that I did with a particularly active and unremorseful thief.[41]

The statistics on the likelihood of recidivism, which is the probability that a thief will re-offend, even after being criminally

---

[40]   https://pinkcollarcrime.com/what-is-pink-collar-crime

[41]   Harris, David. "Steals, and Then Squeals by David Harris." Dentaltown. Accessed July 30, 2019. https://www.dentaltown.com/magazine/article/6366/steals-and-then-squeals.

convicted, are alarming. A 2018 study by the U.S. Department of Justice tracked criminals after being released from prison and found that 45% of them returned to jail in less than a year, 69% got caught within three years, and after five years, 78% of the original offenders had been locked up again.[42] Our justice system does not seem to be able to effect the change in the behavior of transgressors that we hope for.

To understand embezzlement's "frequent fliers" better, it is interesting to compare them to another elite group, those who have stolen more than a million dollars from a single practice. When comparing serial embezzlers to the "Million Dollar Club," several key differences emerge.

Embezzlers who have stolen more than a million dollars are normally trusted, long-term employees who have successfully concealed their stealing for many years. Their embezzlement patterns are sophisticated, well thought out, and these high-achiever thieves have given careful consideration to skirting the scrutiny employed by their victims. They are well-established in the community and display considerable stability in their personal lives.

In contrast, serial embezzlers tend to fit the Narcissistic Sociopath profile discussed in Chapter 4. Their stealing methods tend to be crude (the embezzlement equivalent of throwing a brick through the window of an appliance store), do not normally reflect much awareness of the doctor's control systems, and

---

[42]   Alper, Mario, Matthew R. Durose, and Joshua Markman, 2018 Update on Prisoner Recidivism: A 9-Year Follow-up Period (2005-2014), US Department of Justice 2018

demonstrate a surprising inability to learn from what has gotten them caught previously.

The thief profiled in the Steals then Squeals article mentioned earlier in this chapter worked for over a dozen practices and stole from most of them. Notwithstanding the amount of experience at stealing that she has had, her methods remained (and remain, because I expect she is still stealing somewhere) unsophisticated. Between this lack of skill when stealing and her observable narcissism, she typically got caught quickly, and often within three to six months of being hired. Put another way, this is a person who has been caught stealing more than twelve times! Her true talent lies in convincing a prospective employer not to bother with a proper background workup along the lines discussed in Chapter 22; she is really, at best, a mediocre thief.

Serial embezzlers also tend to have a precarious and peripatetic existence; they will change jobs, living accommodations, cities, and even domestic partners much more frequently than most, often leaving carnage in their wakes. They tend to rent rather than own, have little in the way of savings, and live in a way that most of us would consider to be unstable.

Cash

Another comment that I often hear from dentists relative to their probability of being victims is "I don't take in much cash." When practice owners limit their visualization of embezzlement to the theft of $20 bills, it is easy to underestimate their exposure to embezzlement.

Many dentists do not realize how easy it is for a thief to cash checks payable to someone else, or that other forms of payment like electronic funds transfers and credit card payments can also be hijacked. In the interest of not educating would-be thieves, we will not get too specific here, but it should suffice to say that we encounter non-cash theft in our cases every week.

Second, I have had to gently point out to many dentists that ultimately, they have no idea how much cash is handed over by patients. All that the doctor can measure is how much cash is turned over by staff or what is recorded as being received in the practice management software, which isn't necessarily the same amount as what patients paid. Also, let's not forget that a staff member has various tools to influence how a specific patient pays. If I worked in your practice and wanted to increase the percentage of payments made in cash, I assure you that I could.

Virtual Credit Cards

In addition to the possibility of theft from other payment types, a relatively new form of payment has been more or less forced on dental offices by insurance companies. It is called a virtual credit card, sometimes abbreviated as "VCC."

When an insurance company pays you by VCC, they provide a prepaid credit card number with the Explanation of Benefits for a patient. Your practice receives payment by entering that prepaid card number into your merchant terminal.

While VCCs present a convenient and low-cost way for insurance companies to pay claims, VCCs are a bad idea for you on several levels. First, in addition to the preferred provider adjustment you are probably already surrendering to these insurance companies, you will lose a further amount in the 2-3% fee that your merchant processing company charges you. And if that isn't enough, there are plenty of ways for an enterprising thief to monetize a VCC payment. In the words of former First Lady Nancy Reagan, "Just say no." While several insurance companies will default to this payment option, they cannot **require** you to be paid by VCC. If you are receiving VCC payments, send a letter to the insurance company sending them and tell the company that you wish to be paid by check.

The Perils of Altruism

One surprising statistic that emerged from the 2019 CDP Survey was that, when asked what the victim's response was to the embezzlement to which they had been subjected, only 64.56% of respondents terminated the perpetrators. Therefore, more than 35% of the people caught embezzling kept their jobs![43] More than 25% of employees were given a warning but allowed to keep their jobs, with the action taken not specified in the remaining 10% of cases, which generously might mean that the employee quit on their own.

Of all the crazy things that we have seen dentists do in three decades of working with them, failing to fire an embezzling employee is the most bizarre. There is no way that an employee who steals from you should still have a job, ever. It doesn't matter

---

[43]   American Dental Association. (2019). 2018 CDP Survey on Employee Theft in the Dental Practice. *Center for Dental Practice*

whether they cry and beg for forgiveness, promise never to do it again, or let you know that their dog just died; when someone has stolen from you, sooner or later, the circumstances that pushed that person over the edge will reoccur. These people are ticking time bombs in your practice. Do what you know is right and let them go. If you feel merciful, there are ways to show them kindness, but continuing their employment with you should not be one of them.

The Get-Out-Of-Jail-Free Card

If you have ever played the board game Monopoly, you know exactly what this item is. It's a card that allows you to escape a punishment that is part of the game.

Some embezzlers also have acquired immunity; they have knowledge about their doctor that, if made public, would cause serious trouble for that dentist. The employee correctly reasons that, if the dentist ever confronts them about their stealing, when the embezzler reveals what he or she knows about the dentist along with a thinly veiled threat to expose their boss, the dentist will quickly decide that punishing the embezzler is not a good idea.

Does this amount to blackmail on the part of the employee? Yes, it does, and I'll discuss blackmail (which in some states is referred to as extortion) from a different perspective in Chapter 28.

Is the employee likely to succeed in blackmailing the dentist? The outcome depends on what compromising information the employee has, but because the dentist normally has a lot more to lose than the embezzler, the embezzler will probably prevail.

What are some of the things that a dentist can do that can render them impotent to deal with embezzlement? Here is a non-exhaustive list of possibilities:

- Cheating on your income taxes in a way that is visible to your staff.
- Cutting corners with dental insurance. These liberties could include waiving co-payments, billing insurance for services different than the work that was actually performed, or billing services for a provider other than the one who did the work (for example, if one provider is in-network with a PPO but another provider did the work).
- Having an extra-marital affair with a staff member, or even with the embezzler.[44]

I remember many years ago when a dentist friend asked me for advice when buying a practice. The seller was in his late 60s

---

[44] In case you are wondering how the rules work in this area, insurance claims provide for two entities. They are the "billing dentist" and the "treating dentist." The billing dentist is the entity that "owns" the payment for the claim, and the treating dentist is the practitioner that touched the patient. For example, when a patient is treated by an associate dentist, the practice owner is the billing dentist, and the associate is the treating dentist. You can make whatever entity is entitled to payment as the billing dentist, but the treating dentist must always be the dentist who performed the treatment or supervised the team member that provided the treatment. Misrepresenting the treating dentist to avoid credentialing issues, or for any other reason, constitutes insurance fraud. If you have questions about this area, a great resource in this area is my friend Dr. Roy Shelburne (https://royshelburne.com/).

and was a well-respected dentist and a pillar of his community. My friend's problem was that the selling dentist was insistent that my friend give one of the practice's hygienists a long-term, non-cancellable employment contract, and my friend was concerned about being forced to take this commitment on.

Being the professional cynic that I am, I realized what was really happening, and I let my friend in on the seller's secret, which the seller sheepishly confirmed in a meeting with us. He had been having an extramarital affair with the (much younger) hygienist for years. With her paramour about to sell his practice, the hygienist delivered an ultimatum about going to the seller's wife to reveal the affair unless he arranged long-term employment for her.

My friend took the position that this hygienist's financial security was the seller's problem and not his and simply deducted an amount commensurate with the locked-in amount committed to the hygienist from what he was prepared to pay for the practice. While this story still makes me chuckle, it displays the corner into which you can find yourself painted when someone holds something over you.

One of our core values at Prosperident is that we completely support our clients. This belief means that we never judge the moral choices they make.

However, just like this dentist trying to sell his practice with his affair with the hygienist pressuring him, some decisions you make can have implications well beyond what you expected. And with some of the embezzlers I have encountered, I certainly would not put it past them to entice their doctor into a compromising position.

6

How Secure is My Practice Management Software?

A couple of the most frequently asked questions by doctors regarding practice management software are:

- Is there a brand of practice management software that is better at protecting a doctor against embezzlement?
- What is the most secure software?

This question is like asking whether one hammer is safer to use than another. All hammers have the potential to be safe if used properly and the potential to cause grievous harm if they are not.

How is Practice Management Software Built?

Let's start by looking at your software in a way that is slightly different than how you normally would. Your practice management software really consists of two parts. A relational database has "data tables" containing all the information on your practice. Data tables include patient master information such as name, address, and phone number, as well as treatment records, receivables balances, and so on. The database programming languages used are commercial programs made by big companies like Microsoft and Oracle and licensed to the company that makes your practice management software. The most common database language used in practice management software is SQL, which stands for Structured Query Language.

The second part of practice management software is an interface, or "front end" that allows you and your staff to interact with the database in an organized and hopefully user-friendly fashion.

Data Integrity

What is sometimes behind this question is fear on the part of the dentist posing the question that a clever staff member could somehow bypass the front end of the software and directly make edits to the database or edit the audit trail to erase evidence of wrongdoing.

Since every modern practice management software contains an "audit trail," transactions made through the front end are always visible, whereas edits made directly to the database, not using the software's front end might not be.

I'll put your mind at ease on this one. **Reading** information from the database without using the practice management software's interface isn't hard for someone with a computer science background and some database skills. Accessing databases is something that we do regularly in the course of our investigations.

However, **editing** the data in the data tables is a much more difficult undertaking. Without dragging you into a lot of detail about database architecture and checksums, I can tell you that doing this is very difficult in any modern practice management software. The result of someone trying to make a direct edit is likely that the software will report a "checksum" error indicating corruption to the database, which will require some resuscitation by the support department of the software company to run.

I'm not saying that editing your data in some other way than using the interface can't be done, but this would take someone with PhD-level computer knowledge.

If the Integrity of the Database is Secure, Where Does the Danger Originate?

You've heard the saying from gun advocates that "guns don't kill people; people do." I'll say the same thing here. Most embezzlement occurs not because of inherent weaknesses in practice management software but because human practice owners fail to apply sufficient supervision and common sense to how their practice management software is deployed.

Unfortunately, there is no such thing as embezzlement-proof software. All practice management software is designed with built-in safeguards, but then most practice owners neutralize many of the security features. There is always an inherent tradeoff between controls and efficiency.

For example, it is possible to set up practice management software so that the practice owner is the only person permitted to authorize credit adjustments to patient accounts. While, in theory, this is safer than allowing staff members to adjust without the doctor's approval, it is operationally cumbersome to have staff continuously interrupting the doctor when adjustment transactions need to be authorized. Most offices find the safest options unwieldy and end up deliberately bypassing some of the built-in safety features of their software for the sake of convenience.

Maddeningly, when new practice management software is installed, typically, the default setup disables many of the security features available, and enabling these features requires specific action on the part of the practice. The reason that the companies that make the software take this approach is understandable. With unfamiliar practice management software, higher security settings inevitably prompt more calls to the software maker's support line. When someone new to a particular software discovers that something they are trying to do is blocked, the next step is usually to call the software's technical support department to ask for help. To reduce user frustration and manage support costs, software companies normally turn off many security features in the default setup.

Administrator Privileges

Practice management software invariably follows a hierarchical setup; the administrator account can access every feature in the software and change any security setting, and the privileges granted to other users are subsets of the administrator's privileges.

Granting someone permissions beyond what is required to perform their functions is never a good idea. Setting privileges appropriately merits some study so that, for example, a recall coordinator does not end up with the (unnecessary for their duties) ability to post adjustments or make write-offs.

While this seems like an obvious statement, the granting of administrative privileges to team members should be done extremely carefully. We see far too many offices where the practice owner isn't sure which staff members have top-level privileges in practice management software.

We recommend that in a practice with less than 10 staff, only the doctor (and the doctor's spouse if he or she works in the practice) should have administrative privileges. In larger offices, it may be necessary for the office manager to also have this feature.

Staff "Borrowing" Administrator Privileges

The bad news is that having a severely restricted user account will not stop a determined embezzler. All the built-in security features in practice management software become irrelevant when an employee obtains your "administrator" access code or password.

This access can happen when you leave your workstation unattended without logging out or when a staff member manages to get your password. The methods used for obtaining your password will not be detailed here, but it usually is not difficult for a motivated staff member to acquire an administrator password.

Here are a few protective steps you should take. First, change your own password regularly, at intervals of no more than three months. Some practice management software allows you to make a setting that periodically forces password changes; however, if a staff member has obtained your administrative password, they can override this setting, which means that the software will no longer prompt you.

Whether or not your software enforces regular password changes, set a reminder elsewhere for yourself at three-month intervals to change it. Regularly changing your password does not prevent abuse if your password is compromised, but it limits the damage resulting from such a compromise. Staff members need to change their passwords at similar intervals.

Choosing Passwords

You should never share your own password with anyone in your office and don't fall into the trap of using the same password for everything you do. Using the same password for your Amazon account that you for your administrator's account in practice management software is begging for it to be compromised.

It's slightly humorous to look online at the lists of most popular passwords. The most common lists normally include "123456", "qwerty," and "password." Almost as bad is to use your birthdate, spouse's middle name, or dog's name. Make sure that yours is a random collection of letters, digits, and characters.

I know that it can be a daunting task to keep track of the passwords you use in various places. Happily, the software is available (often called "wallets") to store your various passwords securely. And please don't write your password down on paper somewhere or allow staff to do the same with their passwords. I have gone into several offices and looked under front-desk keyboards, only to find the workstation owner's password written on a post-it note that had been stuck to the bottom of the keyboard. Your staff may grumble a bit about periodically needing to learn a new password, and this will not stop passwords from being revealed, but it will certainly limit the damage if one is compromised.

"We Keep the Passwords on File"

I have also encountered offices where someone, often the office manager, requires every staff member to write down and provide their password for the practice management software, which the office manager then keeps in a locked drawer. This practice is misguided. Removal or disabling a user account in practice management software can be done using an administrator account and does not require knowledge of that user's password. Therefore, there is no supervisory requirement to have everyone's password.

Also, if someone forgets their password, each software has a means for recovery, so recording a staff member's password is not needed for this purpose either.

With a password comes accountability, and that accountability is undermined when more than one person has that password. If embezzlement does take place, when the finger is pointed at a specific staff member, the suspect will quickly point out that they are not the only person with access to this user account. A compromised password can make an investigator's task more difficult by creating some element of doubt as to who made transactions in your software.

However, embezzlement is not simply the act of "cooking the books"; there is also an underlying improper flow of money. If we can establish who received the stolen funds, we can overcome the issue of compromised passwords. However, if we cannot trace stolen funds, password security compromised by your office policy may render your case difficult to pursue.

Two User Accounts for the Practice Owner

We recommend that practice owners should have two user accounts for themselves in the practice management software. One account should have administrator powers, and the other should have the same level of capability as your receptionists' accounts. I probably do not need to tell you that these two accounts should not share a common password.

When I look at how dentists personally use their practice management software, many of the tasks they perform do not require administrator privileges, which are needed infrequently.

The receptionist-level account should be the one you are logged in on most of the time. Log in with your administrator account only when you need to do something requiring administrative authority. The advantage this approach offers is this - while walking away from a computer you have logged in to is still not a good idea, and your computer should be set to log you out automatically after a few minutes of inactivity, there can be far less damage caused if the account in which you are logged in has no higher level of authority than your front-desk machines. On the other hand, leaving a terminal that is logged in with administrator privileges is dangerous.

The "Unicode"

It never fails to astound me that there are still practices where there is one practice management software user account shared by everyone in the practice. Having a single user account means that every staff member has administrative authority in your practice management software. It also makes it more challenging to determine which team member is responsible for any given transaction and more difficult to secure the practice management software when someone leaves the practice.

Every team member, without exception, needs to have their own user account. Your practice should also have a firm policy prohibiting sharing passwords or using someone else's account or using a terminal when logged in with someone else's user name. Password policies will not deter dishonest employees, but they prevent honest team members from becoming unwitting accomplices.

Remote Access

Many practices allow staff members to use a remote access capability to log in to the practice management software from outside the office.

While I recognize the convenience of this (particularly if you live in a part of the country where your staff needs to cancel patients due to adverse weather), allowing staff to have remote access to your software can make detecting embezzlement more difficult. I'll be discussing in Chapter 20 how thieves like to have "alone time" in the office. If remote access is not available, to achieve this means that they must be physically present to do their dirty work, and a burglar alarm system makes this trackable. Thieves gaining their alone time through remote access are much more difficult to monitor.

I have no objection to the practice owner having remote access, and there may be times when staff need temporary remote access (such as the COVID shutdown that took place in 2020). Still, ongoing access is not something we recommend.

What complicates this issue is that remote access software has become far easier to install than it once was. A decade ago, creating remote access probably required the assistance of your IT company. In contrast, now, most remote access software will self-install and create whatever exception it needs in your practice's firewall to operate. This ease of installation means that a staff member can install unauthorized remote access without involving your IT company. It is a really good idea to ask your IT company to periodically conduct a sweep to look for unauthorized remote access software. We have encountered several instances where an employee, after being fired, continued to have access to the practice's computer system.

If you are part of the growing movement toward cloud-based practice management software, remote access exists in the very nature of cloud software. Most cloud-based practice management software has addressed this and will allow you to limit logging in to certain IP Addresses so that you can log in from home, but your staff cannot.

Can a Thief "Houseclean" the Evidence?

One concern that many clients articulate is that the thief will get the idea that they are about to get caught and somehow clean up the software to remove all traces of their malfeasance. This isn't quite how it works. Every practice management software keeps something called an "audit trail" or "audit log" that records every single transaction that is made. When someone tries to cover their defalcations, the audit trail will capture both the original fraudulent transactions and those made to try to hide what was done. For a trained investigator, this has the opposite effect of what the thief intends and ends up making what was done considerably more conspicuous. Accordingly, you do not need to worry about a stealing staff member devoting a weekend to a cleanup party that makes their work invisible because they suddenly got spooked; an attempt to conceal what has been done will both be conspicuous to a trained investigator and will convey a guilty intent.

Most practice management software makes it difficult to delete the file that contains the audit trail or to change the software settings so that an audit trail is no longer kept. The former requires considerable computer knowledge, and the latter normally requires written authorization to be provided to the maker of the software.

If you suspect embezzlement, for the reasons discussed in Chapter 27, it is still important to keep your suspicions from being evident to staff because there are other protective actions they might take, but at the same time, you do not need to worry about a software cover-up.

Backups

Backing up your practice management software, and any other vital computer records, should follow the 3-2-1 rule. You should have three copies of your data, on two different devices, with one of them offsite. I remember the days when backups were done on physical media like tape drives. Cloud storage has made backing up your data so much easier.

Your Alarm System

I hope that your practice has an alarm system. If it doesn't, get one installed.

Similarly, to practice management software, your burglar alarm system needs a unique code for each member of your team.

One important benefit of having an alarm and properly assigned codes is that if someone is coming into your practice at unusual times, you can pinpoint who that person is.

Using a "Unicode" shared by everyone eliminates this ability. It can also prompt poor security habits, especially because when a staff member leaves or is fired, many practices do not bother changing a Unicode because everyone would need to learn a new alarm code, which is not the case with individually assigned codes, where only the departing employee's code is withdrawn.

You should ask the alarm company to email you the "access log" monthly. As we will discuss in Chapter 20, thieves like to be alone when stealing, and a five-minute review of the access log each month will tell you if someone is accessing the practice at unexpected times.

The precautions in this chapter do not take much time or create major inconvenience for people, and they go a long way toward protecting your practice.

7

My Spouse is My Office Manager

Let's tackle one of the "elephants in the room" when talking about dental practice embezzlement. Some dentists are fortunate enough to have a spouse who manages their practice. Often, this is one of the best protection plans you can implement to fight embezzlement because normally, your spouse's economic interests are perfectly aligned with your own. The one exception to this alignment happens when your spouse decides that he or she is going to leave you.

When your spouse, who also manages your office, decides to end your marriage, and before they announce this to you, it may dawn on them that their short-term income security is in jeopardy.

Eventually, they can expect to receive spousal support and child support if they are the custodial parent. However, interim (and for that matter, final) support arrangements take time to work their way through divorce court and become active. While your spouse is waiting for this to happen, they need to make new living arrangements, all the while expecting to be cut off from the income they used to earn managing your practice, plus they will have the added expense of a divorce attorney. Unless your soon-to-be ex-spouse has savings or investments of their own to draw on while things get sorted out, they may feel pressure to do what must be done to set aside the money they expect to need. Sadly, embezzlement is often what these people see as their best option.

Since most practice owners do not feel the need to impose guardrails on a spouse's actions in a practice, if a spouse does decide to embezzle, they can do so with impunity.

Embezzlement by a spouse who is not planning to divorce the dentist is not common, but it can happen. One case of spousal embezzlement I witnessed involved a dentist whose new wife had emigrated from an economically developing country. She wanted to send money back to her family, but she did not want to ask her husband, the dentist, for help. Instead, she used her new position as his office manager to steal the money she wanted to send her family. Predictably, the doctor's discovery of his wife's misappropriations ended their marriage.

Studies suggest that 40% of first marriages, and 60% of second marriages, in the US will end in divorce, so pre-divorce embezzlement is not a phenomenon to which we can be oblivious.[45]

---

[45]　Lewis, Henry F. "Divorce Statistics in the United States and California." Family Law Attorney - Oakland, CA - Gardner & Lewis, LLP, October 9, 2018. https://www.michaelagardner.net/blog/2018/10/09/divorce-statistics-in-the-united-193973.

Sometimes, a "dental couple" gets divorced but continues working together. This may provide a convenient solution for both parties, because the dentist continues to need an office manager and the spouse still needs an income. However, if you decide to leave a spouse who is divorcing you in their position in your practice, please consider that their economic interests no longer parallel yours, and that you need to put the safeguards in place that would apply to any other arm's length employee.

8

Dentists Can Embezzle, Too

One thing that always surprises my audiences is when I recount situations where the thief in a practice is a dentist. While most dentists can understand how team members decide to embezzle, for many doctors, the idea that a professional brother or sister practitioner, sharing a similar education and the same code of ethics, would steal is inconceivable. And yet it happens – roughly 10% of our cases involve what we call "fratricide," and two of our most senior investigators spend most of their time on this work. Given that only 14% of dental practices are group practices, the amount of improper activity between doctors is shockingly high.

While there are countless variants, this stealing usually takes the form of a doctor embezzling from their partners in a group practice or a seller of a practice embellishing the practice's performance when valuing it before a sale.

I remember a phone call I received from a specialist a few years ago. After a brief introduction, he explained that he practiced with another member of the same specialty and that he and his partner had an "arrangement" whereby, when patients paid cash, the caller and his partner would pocket the money and not report it as income to the Internal Revenue Service.

This tactic is not something that I would recommend, but I was curious about where this conversation was going. The doctor then made his next statement, the one that rendered me temporarily speechless: "The reason that I am calling you, David, is that I believe that my partner is stealing more than I am."

As it turned out, he was right, and his partner was taking differential advantage of their unwritten arrangement. I will mention that considerable effort went into wording the final report for this investigation, so as not to flag the creative "tax planning" that was taking place.

I saw another two-doctor specialist practice where one of the owners was planning on going out on his own. He ran a lot of the startup expenses for his new practice through the existing practice and had some of the staff (who were being paid by both doctors) making calls to referring dentists to let them know about his new arrangement. He even scheduled a lavish marketing event to kick off his new practice and charged the full cost to the existing practice.

Every group practice has some formula for the allocation of income to the dentists. This relationship may be one of associateship, multiple owners, or both. If there are multiple owners, there are various possible models for sharing income, ranging from sharing expenses only (which I like to think of as the "eat what you kill" model) to models where income gets homogenized on some basis between the owners.

Regardless of the arrangement, sometimes one or more doctors believe that the compensation formula is unfair to them. Such was the case with a three-doctor practice I worked with early in my career. In interviews with the three doctors, I discovered that each believed that he was under-compensated and that the income allocation model was unfair to him. Although this was a mathematical impossibility, each of the three had the belief that the other two were taking advantage of them.

Setting up a model that allocates income fairly to owners of a group practice is challenging. What confounds many of the income distribution formulae is a change in circumstances that was not envisaged when they were designed.

I remember seeing one three-doctor practice where the fixed costs, such as rent and salaries, were "unitized," which means allocated to each doctor based on their share of the total production. This approach made total sense for the two younger doctors because the other more experienced doctor was the highest biller and accordingly ended up shouldering a higher share of the practice's fixed costs.

However, when the senior doctor was a few years from retirement, he began slowing down. When this happened, the formula had the effect of redirecting the responsibility for fixed overhead from the senior doctor to his younger colleagues. At retirement, the senior doctor sold his practice to a new graduate, who at the time was unable to reproduce even what his predecessor billed while coasting into retirement. This decrease in output prompted a further reallocation of overhead to the two other owners. From the perspective of these two dentists, nothing had changed in how they were practicing, and yet they saw their allocation of the practice's overhead gradually increase from 60% of the practice's total outlays to 85%.

Normally it takes unanimous consent in a practice to change a compensation formula, which means that whoever would be adversely affected by a proposed change is unlikely to bless it.

It is not hard to visualize how this feeling of exploitation provides a dentist with the ability to rationalize, which, as you know, is a necessary precondition for stealing.

While the prevalence of dentists embezzling is modest compared with the frequency with which staff embezzles, it happens enough that it must be considered in any group practice arrangement.

In many group practices, dentists adopt roles that reflect their strengths and interests. For example, it is common for one dentist to become the "clinical lead" and another to assume leadership of the practice's business function. This specialization of responsibility is a convenient division of the workload of running a practice. It also means that the dentist who is looking after the practice's business affairs is unsupervised and therefore has ample opportunity to steal.

Dentists who steal do so for the same reasons as everyone else; need and greed. They are either in dire financial circumstances and look to embezzlement to bail them out, or they believe the compensation formula being used is unfair to them and address that feeling by stealing.

If you do practice in a group, be aware that, no matter how odious you find the concept to be, stealing by another practice owner is a possibility and that some level of transparency and oversight over a partner looking after the financial affairs of the practice is needed.

9

Multi-location Practices and DSOs

While it is easy to understand the vulnerability of solo and small group practices, it is tempting to believe that larger practice organizations, which generally have better controls, professional management, and centralized services like recare booking and payment processing, should be less prone to embezzlement.

This belief does not hold out in practice. I remember speaking at a conference for group practice owners a few years ago. I was sitting at a table for breakfast with seven attendees at the conference, each of whom owned at least five dental practices. We were talking about my favorite subject, embezzlement. I didn't initiate this, but the doctor sitting next to me conducted a poll among the seven practice owners to see how many times each of them had been embezzled. He started by saying that he wasn't asking **if** they had been embezzled; he was certain that each of them had. What he was asking was **how**

many times. Each of them gave a number, invariably followed by the disclaimer "that I know of." The numbers ranged from two to six times, with the average being a bit more than three.

The math for the underlying probability is like that of coin tosses. If you toss one coin, the chance of it landing on heads is 50%. When you toss two coins at once, the chance of getting at least one head increases to 75%. When you toss four coins, the probability of at least one being a head is 93.75%, and so on. The increased probability of embezzlement from aggregating more and more providers and employees needs to be considered against any difference that a bigger entity's presumably improved control systems might create.

To their credit, larger organizations typically do a better job of oversight than solo practices do. Therefore, as discussed in Chapter 17, reconciliation theft is usually more difficult with a DSO or multi-office practice. However, these entities are still vulnerable to the various games that embezzlers play in practice management software to make that software misrepresent the amount of money that has been collected.

DSOs also have some vulnerabilities that owner-operated practices normally do not have. For example, when functions are centralized, this creates the possibility of embezzlement taking place in a head office department.

DSOs grow in two ways; "de novo" offices that they start from scratch, and "affiliated" offices where the DSO enters a financial relationship with an existing practice.

Affiliation creates some risks. First, there is the possibility that the DSO affiliates with an office where embezzlement is taking place. Given that employees of such an office have probably not been vetted to the standard that the DSO would apply for new hires, and that typically pre-acquisition due diligence does not extend to scrutiny for embezzlement, there is a reasonable possibility that the DSO ends up "buying a problem."

The second issue with affiliation is that the financial arrangements that many DSOs use when affiliating with a practice owner involve some form of "earn-out." In an earn-out, the affiliating dentist is normally paid some money up-front, with some additional compensation paid later and tied to the future performance of the practice. This is normally a separate arrangement from the affiliated dentist's compensation for personal productivity. In other words, an affiliated dentist may receive 30% of collections based on their own collections, plus an additional amount based on the profitability of the practice. Within these two arrangements, there is considerable potential for manipulation.

We recently wrapped up a case where an affiliated dentist manipulated his earnout after affiliating with a large DSO. Without getting into detail, he found a means to shift income from a period when the earnout did not apply to one where it did. The impact was considerable, and the DSO's legal counsel recently told me that the DSO received a payment of $500,000 from the doctor to repay the misappropriation. You must wonder about the motivation for this kind of action. The doctor had a very successful practice and received an above-market purchase price from the DSO. Once the affiliation was in place, by all accounts the DSO treated him extremely fairly. And yet he saw the need to try to cheat the DSO.

Another danger faced by larger enterprises takes place when multiple providers in the same practice have different bases for compensation. For example, picture a practice with two associate dentists where one dentist's contract pays based on amounts collected, and the other associate is paid based on fees billed. Or a scenario where a dentist is paid based on collections next to a hygienist who is paid hourly. It doesn't take much imagination to understand how shifting work between people with different compensation arrangements (or shifting how that work is recorded in practice management software) can increase the combined compensation of these two producers, thus allowing them to turn the asymmetry into an advantage.

And then there is the emotional element. As discussed in Chapter 4, one of the preconditions for embezzlement is the thief's ability to rationalize the act of stealing; something that the embezzler has repeatedly been told is wrong. Some of the rationalizations we discussed in that chapter are probably easier to apply to DSOs and multi-office practices than the more traditional office. In particular, the following rationalizations tend to line up with a thief's perception of the DSO environment in which they practice:

- The practice deserves to be stolen from. This rationalization originates from the concept that the entity being victimized is itself dishonest. I labeled this rationalization **condemning the condemners** and is consistent with how DSOs are sometimes portrayed in the media as big, uncaring, and avaricious, which mirrors how some of the people who work there perceive their employer.

- I only took a little bit, and the organization will not miss it. This reasoning is a **denial of injury** rationalization. It is far easier to construct when someone is stealing from what they view as a faceless, monolithic entity than it is in a single-office practice where the thief must steal from the person who signs their paycheck and works thirty feet away.
- Others are doing it too. In Chapter 4, we labeled this a **claim of relative acceptability/normality.** It is easy to convince yourself that "everyone is doing it" in a big practice and that it is normal or accepted.

In addition to stealing from a larger entity being easier to rationalize than embezzling from a smaller business, bigger practice groups suffer from hubris when it comes to this topic. The "we are big; therefore, we must be smart" overconfidence does not change the fact that, at a fundamental level, they are just a collection of small retail offices that all take payments over the counter and that offer the same set of opportunities to a thief that a one-location practice does.

We have worked for many multi-office practices and DSOs and have encountered many smart, high-quality people there. Refreshingly, they normally appreciate our insight and ability to adopt an embezzler's perspective to see the opportunities that embezzlers might avail themselves of in that organization.

What can a DSO or larger practice do to protect itself? I have a few recommendations:

1. Create a culture of honesty. This core value needs to originate at the organization's executive level and apply to all facets of the operation.
2. Be receptive to whistleblowing. Chapter 4 discussed the reluctance of people working in small entities to come forward with concerns about co-workers. The size of a DSO or multi-office practice may make it easier for an employee to call attention to their concerns. To encourage people to bring their concerns forward, there should be a clearly articulated policy that provides reassurance to prospective whistleblowers.

    One option is to create a reward program for whistleblowers. If this is done, the rewards should be modest and probably not percentage based. The difficulty with rewards calculated on a percentage is that it may take several years before determining how much recovery will be received, and you may want to make a more immediate reward.
3. The separation between balancing and oversight that will be discussed in Chapter 17 is critical. There needs to be financial oversight of individual practices that includes a review of both daily and monthly totals for each practice with banking records and the monitoring of practice management software for improper transactions that could cause the software to misrepresent the amount collected.
4. The team members performing the internal audit function need direct access to each office's practice

management software. Reviewing reports prepared by individual practices is not sufficient.

5. Clearly, the internal audit task is easier if all the entity's practices use the same practice management software. This consistency is easy when growth takes place by opening *de novo* offices and is more complicated when growth takes place by affiliating with existing practices. When growth is done by affiliation, there should be a plan to transition new offices to the "standard" practice management software within a fairly short period.

6. There needs to be an ongoing program where some proportion of a DSO's practices are subjected to an in-depth audit annually. We have worked with several DSOs to design and deliver such audit programs, which often combine some amount of targeting of statistical outliers (e.g., offices with abnormally low collection ratios) with some practices targeted purely at random. These audit programs have several objectives:

    a. To raise the perception of detection in the minds of staff members working in individual offices.

    b. To review selected offices in depth beyond what the DSO could do internally.

    c. To flag weaknesses in internal controls for top management attention.

7. With multiple practices, oversight is far easier if each practice maintains its own bank account, even if only for deposit purposes. When you have five (or 35) practices, dumping daily collections into a single bank account, reconciliation against practice management software

becomes almost impossible. On the other hand, if each practice has its own deposit account, it is much easier to isolate the source of any deficiency.

This requirement does not prevent you from consolidating deposited funds or making disbursements from a central bank account, but it is far simpler if each practice's deposits can be tracked to a single account.

DSOs vary widely in culture and business models. While they are sometimes targets for criticism, they can offer dentists the benefits of highly efficient business models and the ability to focus on clinical dentistry, which explains their success and rapid growth.

10

Protect Yourself as an Associate

While most of this book is oriented toward owners of dental practices, I would be remiss if I didn't address the topic of associate dentists.

Associateship is a wonderful way for dentists to perfect their clinical skills without having to deal with the issues associated with running a practice simultaneously. It also is a good fit for more senior dentists in certain situations. However, it is not without its financial issues.

Associates can become embezzlement victims in several ways. First, they can end up being underpaid relative to what they are entitled. As much as we would prefer to believe that no practice owner would abuse an associate, we sometimes see an avaricious practice owner fiddling with the books to an associate's financial detriment.

At other times, it happens because of mistakes being made at the front desk. For example, if treatment is accidentally coded to the wrong provider, this may end up lowering the associate's pay. Particularly when a one-dentist office adds its first associate, a different mindset is required from front desk staff when posting to practice management software than how things were done before. In a solo practice where hygienists are salaried, it makes no financial difference whether a recall exam is coded to the dentist or the hygienist. For this reason, it is understandable that many small offices aren't used to being careful about certain details. However, when an associate comes on board, the need for more accurate recordkeeping suddenly arises, and sometimes front desk team members and even practice owners fail to realize this. To make it worse, most practice management software defaults to the "dentist of record" when making entries. When an associate is newly added to a practice, this dentist of record is normally the practice owner. Unless staff consistently remember to override this default provider when entering treatment performed by the associate, or payments belonging to this treatment, there is a realistic possibility that the associate will be underpaid.

There is also the possibility that embezzlement is happening at a practice and that one or more associate dentists join with the practice owner in becoming victims.

And finally, buying all or part of a practice where a staff member is stealing can provide a buyer with a difficult and unforeseen introduction to practice ownership, when the buyer suddenly realizes that they need to pay for and invest time in cleaning up a mess left by their predecessor.

Setting Up Associateship Properly

Here are some things that associates can do to protect themselves.

On making an agreement to become an associate, ensure that the agreement provides sufficient access to practice information to ensure that your compensation is being properly determined. Information sharing is always a touchy subject for a practice owner who can understandably be reluctant to give you information that may have commercial value if you establish your own practice nearby or take an associate position with a competitor. However, you need to be firm in insisting that you need sufficient access to the practice management software to confirm that your compensation is correct.

Normally, the compensation formula for an associate is based on one of two measurements; **production**, for which the yardstick can be either gross or net production (i.e., after adjustments), or **collections**.

If your pay is calculated on production, you require day-end production reports from the practice management software that show both your gross production and any adjustments.

If your pay is calculated based on collections, you need those production reports plus collections reports showing who paid and how much. You also need a monthly receivable listing that shows all amounts owing for work performed by you. This report should be "aged" – in other words, it should show how old the amounts owing are. You also need the report showing open insurance claims for your work.

Your agreement should also provide you with access to the "ledger" for each patient for whom you have a balance. The ledger is a summary of individual transactions on a patient's account.

I stress that your right to access this information should be enshrined in your associate agreement, not something left to the practice owner's good faith. If that right isn't expressed in your agreement, you will be in a difficult position later when you think you are being under-compensated, but you do not have the right to access the information necessary to determine whether this is true.

If your compensation is based on collections, your need for information (and therefore your right to it) will extend past the date when you are no longer working in the practice. More than a few associates have lost money because collections that took place after the associate moved on were not shared with the associate.

Your agreement should provide that after you leave the practice, any payments made by a patient or insurance company will be applied to the oldest balance first. This requirement is to prevent a practice owner from "orphaning" your balances and encouraging patients to make payments on amounts that he or she does not have to share with you.

How to keep track

Review the production, adjustments, and collections, if paid on collections, daily. Look at the receivables monthly and compare them to the receivables listing you received the previous month. Some questions to ask yourself when reviewing this information:

In all situations:

1. Did all the patients you saw today show up in the production report?
2. Were the procedures performed today accurately recorded in the production report?
3. Do you understand and agree with all adjustments against production given to the patients you saw today?
4. Were the treatment of external lab bills consistent with your associate agreement?
5. Was the treatment of radiography and recall exams consistent with your associate agreement?

If paid based on collections:

6. Did the front desk collect co-pays in accordance with office policy from all patients who were in today?
7. What efforts are being taken to collect balances for your work that are overdue? Are there any patients you should call yourself? Should any patients be sent to a collection agency? If you think collection efforts on your patients are inadequate, you may wish to discuss this with the practice owner.
8. If insurance claims have been rejected, have they been resubmitted by staff with whatever extra information is needed?

9. Are patients with significant balances being reappointed with you? If yes, why?
10. Do balances age properly? In other words, if an amount was 30 days past due a month ago, and it hasn't been paid, it should now show up in the 60 days past due column.
11. Is the change in receivables for your work reflected in your pay? If receivables decreased by $15,000 this month, you should receive ($15,000 plus collections for this month's work) x your payment percentage.
12. Are payments from patients on whom multiple providers worked being applied to the correct provider? A symptom that this is not being done is when patients have "double balances." This phenomenon means that a patient has a debit (i.e., positive) balance with one provider and a credit (negative) balance with another provider.

Buying a Practice

Many new practice owners have had an unfortunate awakening when they realize that the practice that they just purchased has an embezzlement issue. A second shock ensues when new practice owners realize that the people they thought were protecting them from this eventuality actually have no responsibility. The new owner is left to their own devices to deal with the mess.

Obviously, a dangerous scenario for buying a practice with active embezzlement is when the buyer is unfamiliar with the practice, but it also happens when the new owner has been with the practice for some time as an associate. In many cases, when embezzlement comes to light after a purchase, I expect that the former owner was unaware that stealing was happening. Unfortunately, there are also situations where the former owner knew or suspected that embezzlement was taking place but didn't share that knowledge because he or she wanted the sale to you to go through and thought that you might have been scared away if he or she told you what they knew or suspected.

The other scenario that afflicts buyers is that inaccurate information is provided about the purchase – revenue, number of active patients, the number of new patients per month, etc. Sometimes this is accidental, and at other times it is a deliberate action of the selling dentist looking to extract every possible dollar from the sale. Sadly, in a typical year, we look at dozens of situations where the buyer of a practice retains us to work with their attorneys to determine if the seller has overstated attributes of the practice.

How to Protect Yourself when Buying

Here are some considerations and steps to take when buying a practice:

1. The people who assist you should have specialized dental expertise. Most of us have friends or relatives who are lawyers and accountants, and it is often tempting to use them to represent you in a purchase. No matter how well-intended these people are and how

reasonable their fees may be, there is no substitute for dental-specific expertise when protecting you. A purchase agreement specifically designed for dental transactions will give you better protection than a generic agreement also used to sell car dealerships. While most embezzlement could not be spotted by a CPA doing a pre-purchase financial review, a dental CPA is in a good position to ensure that you are paying a fair price and certainly has a better chance of seeing that something is amiss than a non-dental accountant.

2. The broker doesn't work for you. Normally a broker is hired by and compensated by the seller. The broker normally takes information provided by the seller, uses it to determine a price, and provides you with an information package. Brokers normally stamp a big disclaimer across all their information, indicating that they have not verified or audited it in any way. If the broker is fed incorrect information by the seller, either deliberately or inadvertently, the broker will quickly point to this disclaimer when challenged.

   While I have had the good fortune of working with many knowledgeable and principled brokers, unfortunately, there are a few who behave differently. The brokerage industry is virtually unregulated, which facilitates the antics of the crooked few. Be wary of any broker working for the seller who attempts to isolate you from objective advice or tries to control your due diligence process.

3. One thing that differentiates the sale of dental practices from other big-ticket sales is that most of the time, the "appraisals" used in dentistry are performed by the people selling the practices. Contrast this with, for example, real estate. Real estate appraisals are performed by a separate profession from those who sell properties. Real estate agents may perform "market studies" to help a seller determine the listing price, but only a real estate appraiser does the appraisal that a bank requires for financing, and the appraiser is not allowed to be financially involved in any way in the sale of the property. However, when a broker values a dental practice, a low valuation may translate into a quick sale for a practice broker, and a high valuation will result in a higher commission, so clearly, there is financial involvement on the part of the broker.

   Again, this is not an indictment of the dental brokerage industry, which has many great people and provides a valuable service. However, the buyer of a practice needs to be aware of the lack of independence in a dental practice valuation compared with how real estate works.

4. Do a chart audit. It amazes me how often this step is not done. As well as helping you plan what you are going to do with the resource you just purchased, chart audits can help you spot where the information you have been provided does not make sense, such as when the practice where 4,000 active patients are claimed, but there is only a single hygienist.

5. Review summary information in the practice management software. This information should include historical information about fees charged, adjustments, frequency of procedure codes, and the number of new patient exams. A large part of what you pay when buying a practice is for revenue potential and new patient flow, so you need to understand what has happened according to a practice's practice management software. You may want to enlist the help of a consultant or software trainer to help you make sense of the information.

6. Interview the staff. This process is often a somewhat sensitive area because the selling dentist may not want it publicly known that he or she is selling and certainly does not want to get their staff stirred up if a purchase falls through. The way to make this palatable to a seller is to make it a "condition precedent." This condition means that the buyer and seller have agreed that interviews will occur, but it only happens after there is a signed agreement in place. I can't promise you that this process will allow you to spot an embezzler, but it may help you to identify future problem employees.

7. Be alert for "non-replicable" revenue. Sometimes this comes from a special skill that the selling dentist possesses (such as treating temporomandibular disorders or sleep apnea) that you will not be able to replicate; it may be from his or her ability to charge above-market fees for certain procedures. It may even be from some non-clinical business activity carried on

by the dentist, such as speaking fees he or she earns or even revenue from some kind of multi-level marketing. As much as we might think this will not happen, another source of non-replicable revenue exists when a dentist improperly bills insurance.

If the broker has failed to segregate this revenue when performing a valuation, you may end up paying for revenue you can't possibly earn. A comparison between revenue according to practice management software and revenue from accountant-prepared financial statements may give some indication of this, as will looking at revenue by procedure code from the practice management software.

8. Understand the basic flaw in most practice valuations. Many valuations use past performance as a surrogate for the future and apply a multiplier to a "normalized" version of practice profitability.

   While this approach makes sense most of the time, it disadvantages a buyer purchasing from an "overtreater". By doing work earlier than most dentists would, this dentist has essentially borrowed from the patients' future dental needs. The dentist purchasing this practice can pay a high price (based on past revenue and profits) and struggle to fill his or her chair because the already heavily restored patients do not need much treatment.

9. Have part of the purchase price held back and payable later. When funds are held back in this fashion, the money should be funded at closing and placed in

escrow, with a specific escrow agreement dealing with it. This escrow is not the same as the seller agreeing to "hold paper" to provide part of the financing for a purchase, which has a different timeline and terms.

Deferring the payment of some portion of the purchase price provides some incentive for the seller to follow through on future commitments. This holdback is particularly important when the seller has agreed not to compete within a certain radius. If escrow funds are still being held, the seller is unlikely to break this restrictive covenant.

Also, the final accounting for a purchase cannot normally be concluded in real-time at closing and needs some time to be finalized.

Negative financial information sometimes emerges after the purchase is concluded. If the seller has already received the full purchase price, the buyer's position is much weaker than if part of the purchase price can be "frozen" until the dispute is resolved.

10. Have a proper, dental-specific agreement. A good agreement is much more likely when using an attorney who specializes in dental transactions. The agreement should do a few important things:

    a. Provide "representations" of any key financial metrics on which you are relying. For example, if you have been told that there are 4,000 active patients and if this number is important to you, this number should be stated in the agreement. Don't assume that because this information is on a broker's "cut sheet," that you have any ability to hold the seller to it. As mentioned, if the information provided by the broker is inaccurate, the seller will blame the broker, and the broker will blame the seller.

b. Define key terms. Metrics such as "active patients" need to be defined. If they are not, you will never be successful in getting a partial refund for a deficiency. To correctly determine the number of active patients, you first need a clear and operable definition. The legal system relies heavily on precise wording to express the intent of parties to an agreement, and you should never bet the farm on the concept that everyone can agree on whether a specific patient is active or not.

c. Address copayments specifically. Many buyers have had bought practices without realizing that the seller was habitually not collecting copayments. This practice puts the buyer in the terrible position of either having to continue the seller's unethical behavior or to deal with a revolt from patients who are suddenly asked to pay for a portion of their dentistry. The seller's handling of copayments should be made clear in the agreement so that you do not get this kind of surprise.

d. The seller should specifically state that he or she is not aware of embezzlement in the practice and has not consulted any professional concerning embezzlement in the practice in the past two years or if a professional has been consulted, outline who and when. If the seller has had embezzlement concerns, this might be a time to insist on the seller having a proper investigation done, which should be at her or his expense and before the sale closes.

11. Understand potential conflicts in the purchasing process. I previously mentioned that the broker is paid by, and answerable to, the seller, but you should also be wary of any other advisor working for both parties. While legal ethics normally prohibit an attorney from representing both sides in a transaction, the same restrictions may not apply to an accountant or a banker. I'm not suggesting that there is often a large conspiracy formed to fleece a prospective purchaser of his or her money, but when you look to your advisors for objective advice, a past relationship with the seller may cloud this objectivity.

For many dentists, moving from being an associate to a practice owner represents an important milestone in their dental career. I hate to see what should be such a joyous event smirched by the horrible realization that what you acquired was not what you thought you were getting. Following the steps in this chapter is a great way to minimize this risk and protect yourself. Feel free to reach out to us if you have any concerns.

11

What Does Not Stop Embezzlement, and Why

There are plenty of articles published each year with titles like "Four Things You Can Do to Prevent Embezzlement in Your Practice." Many of these embezzlement articles are written by someone working in the dental field, but the authors often lack the daily contact with embezzlement that my team has. This lack of contact causes most of these authors to write from "intuition" or perform online research, making their articles a recapitulation of what others have written on the subject. This approach means that certain myths get passed from one author to another instead of dying out.

While these authors have the very best of intentions, they consistently make a couple of critical errors.

I'll make a bold statement – the concept of prevention doesn't exist. Let me explain why.

First, the people writing articles of this kind start from a manifestly incorrect premise. They assume that what controls other types of crime works to prevent or deter embezzlement as well. Chapter 4 discussed the fatal limitations of this assumption, which I sometimes refer to as the "Hard Target Fallacy."

Increasing the perceived difficulty of stealing works well in deterring opportunistic criminals like house burglars or car thieves because it is very easy for them to switch targets to one that looks easier. However, switching victims for embezzlement is a huge undertaking. By its nature, embezzlement requires the thief to have detailed knowledge about the victim's habits and thought processes. Therefore, rather than seeking another victim and accepting the delay in stealing that will ensure from changing employers, embezzlers will simply keep working through possible modalities for stealing until they find one that is not thwarted by the doctor's control systems. The thief is aided by the sizeable amount of "how-to" information that is available online. In a rush to display their knowledge, several people who write these articles about embezzlement give far more detail about specific methodologies for embezzlement than they should. This information is at least as helpful to would-be embezzlers as YouTube videos are to me when I need to do a complicated repair on my bicycle.

The flaw in the "hard target" logic should be apparent. Given that it is virtually impossible to convince an embezzler to choose a different victim, how effective are the well-intended and often published articles entitled "Four Things That Will Prevent Embezzlement" as a road map to stopping internal theft?

Second, many who speak or write on this topic underestimate the motivation and creativity of embezzlers. People embezzle to address a perceived need. As discussed in Chapter 3, sometimes, the need is financial, and other times, it is emotional.

In either case, "need" is a powerful motivation, and you should not expect a few minor obstacles to steer an embezzler toward honesty. As for creativity, my team and I have been investigating embezzlement for thirty years, and during that time, my investigators have seen hundreds of embezzlement methodologies employed, and we still encounter new ones regularly. Some of them are basic, and others are jaw-dropping in their cleverness and creativity.

It might help to think of the problem this way: if you picture your dental practice as having many embezzlement "doors," and if you can find the time to lock four (or ten or fifty) of those doors, a would-be thief still has many options and will surely find an ingress.

I am not suggesting that there is nothing to be done to control embezzlement. On the contrary, you have powerful tools available to make embezzlement easier to spot, minimize its damage, and facilitate the investigative process. Chapter 30 will offer some simple yet effective strategies to gain the upper hand over those who might steal from you. They just require a slightly different way of thinking than what is offered by these articles written by the "well-intentioned dabblers."

There are other reasons why controls are ineffective against embezzlement. First, there is an inherent tradeoff between controls and operational efficiency. For example, a division of responsibilities between front-desk staff is often advocated to reduce vulnerability to embezzlement. I do not believe this to be the case, and like almost every control, dividing duties creates inefficiency. Therefore, doing so will increase staff workload, resulting in increased staffing costs or reduced productivity.

Second, many controls and procedures are not performed by the doctor personally; they are really directions given to staff about how to perform their duties. Embezzling employees can usually apply these procedures selectively. I vividly remember speaking at a dental conference about how embezzlers steal checks. Many doctors believe that it is difficult for a thief to cash a check payable to the doctor, and I was outlining how easy it is. One doctor put his hand up and informed me that theft of checks would never happen in his office because the backs of checks are stamped with the words "For Deposit Only" to a specific bank and account number.

Doing this is referred to as making a "conditional endorsement," and it is normally effective; it becomes much more difficult for a third party to negotiate a check that has received a conditional endorsement. The other form of endorsement is an unconditional endorsement; this involves simply signing the back of the check with no specific direction about who can negotiate it next. An unconditional endorsement makes the check payable to the "bearer," which means the person who possesses the check.

The question I asked this doctor was a simple one: "Do you stamp the checks yourself?" His somewhat haughty response was: "Of course not!"

Then I asked my follow-up question: "So why would an embezzler, who by definition does not feel compelled to follow society's rules, ever be expected to follow your procedures, when doing so would cost that embezzler money?" He did not have a good answer.

Let's accept that it is impossible in a dental office to remove *all* embezzlement opportunities without also making it impossible for staff to do their jobs. Furthermore, as I suggested, reducing opportunity carries a financial cost. Since reducing (but not eliminating) opportunities does not commensurately decrease the probability of embezzlement, spending money for this purpose does not make sense.

Does this mean that you are powerless, and that embezzlement is inevitable? Definitely not. It's not hard to eliminate the bottom 50% of thieves and to force more sophisticated embezzlers into higher risk patterns, while simultaneously increasing your probability of detection.

How do you do these things? Keep reading.

12

A Crime of Navigation

Every budding embezzler starts the same way: they begin by studying their environment. They are aided in this process by already having or quickly acquiring a detailed understanding of you and your habits. Successful embezzlers are always good observers of their environments. I like to think of embezzlement as a "crime of navigation," where a thief plans a methodology of stealing designed to skirt around your scrutiny.

Embezzlers usually start their analysis by determining whether the oversight procedure in the practice is properly done (we will discuss how to oversee your practice properly in Chapter 17). Oversight refers to the process where daily or monthly totals generated by your practice management software are compared with external information such as your bank deposit or deposits to your merchant account (when patients pay by credit card.) In other words, it is really the supervision of the daily "balancing" activity carried out by the front desk staff or the office manager. Frequently we find in practices is that only partial oversight is done or that balancing it is left completely in the hands of a staff member with no oversight from the practice owner.

If the embezzler determines that the oversight process is flawed, this revelation grants them the liberty to steal without any particular need to conceal it, which we call reconciliation theft. In other words, methodologies employed in this situation can be rudimentary and within the grasp of even employees who are less than gifted intellectually.

On the other hand, if the oversight process is carried out properly, a thief will undoubtedly have observed this and will not do something that results in a visible "out of balance" situation. The trick for doing this is to find a way to lower patient account balances and to do so in a way that does not cause your practice management software to believe that a corresponding amount of money should be deposited into your practice's bank account.

To protect practice owners, I will not go into detail here about how this is done but let me assure you that it is possible. Over the years, our investigators have seen many clever and creative methodologies for fooling the "double-entry accounting" that is implicit in practice management software.

In a lot of the initial calls dentists make to us, there is an undertone of self-blame. Once a practice owner realizes the (unguarded) pathway that their embezzler has exploited, their regretful comment is that they should never have left that opportunity open.

Consider, for example, situations where a team member has been entrusted with making bank deposits with no oversight by the practice owner. Inevitably, in some of these practices, not all the money that leaves the practice arrives at the bank. In other words, these offices are victimized because a staff member diverted part of the deposit.

On finding out that this is what happened to them, many dentists quickly jump to conclude that they would not have been victimized if they had only made the bank deposits themselves. The pseudo-experts on embezzlement (I referred to them as "well-intentioned dabblers" in Chapter 11) tend to reinforce this kind of thinking and often suggest that the doctor should make the bank deposits personally. I refer to this as a "denial of opportunity" approach.

While intuitive, this line of thinking ignores one basic fact. If the practice owner made the bank deposits herself or himself, this would not affect the embezzler's need for money. The result is to leave the practice with an unrequited thief, who would then be actively looking for and would almost certainly find another way to steal from the practice.

Against this, you need to consider the value of the lost time to the doctor by visiting the bank daily, which is a menial task. Rather than making the bank deposit personally, I would prefer to see the doctor spend a couple of minutes using their online banking to compare the amount that went into the bank against their practice management software or outsource that oversight responsibility to an external bookkeeper.

In addition to being creative, thieves are also adaptive. If you change your pattern, this will also not change the thief's need for money, so expect your thief to adapt their stealing model in response and navigate their changed environment.

13

Can Financial Ratios Detect Embezzlement?

I've encountered plenty of accountants and practice management consultants who are convinced that it is possible to spot embezzlement by having a close look at a practice's financial ratios.

While ratios can provide lots of useful information on running your practice, and I'd never suggest that looking at key performance indicators is a bad idea, using ratios to detect embezzlement will not work. If it were possible to detect embezzlement through ratio analysis, we would do that instead of the much more in-depth and labor-intensive process that we follow.

The biggest issue is that many advisors do not realize how much dental practice embezzlement takes place in the form of skimming (i.e., theft of revenue) compared with other forms of theft.

Here are the issues in using revenue analysis for detection:

1. If a theft follows the most common pattern, theft of revenue, the dollars stolen are small relative to total revenue. Therefore, the impact on ratios where revenue is the denominator is minimal.

   For example, one ratio that many observers watch closely is the staff expense ratio (staff costs divided by revenue.)

   Let's assume that a practice where the staff expense ratio is 28% hires someone who starts stealing 2% of revenue. This theft will increase the staff expense ratio to 28.57% (calculated as 28% divided by 98%). Given that revenue fluctuates and there is a bit of inherent variability in payroll costs from factors like pay raises and staff turnover, it will be extremely challenging to separate the change caused by this embezzlement from normal variability.

   However, if someone is stealing the same 2% by tampering with payroll, now the staff expense ratio would increase from 28% to 30%, which probably would be noticeable. This visibility is probably why we seldom see large amounts of money stolen via payroll theft.

2. Some ratios are calculated on a time interval that is too short to be meaningful. For example, looking at supplies expense compared to revenue produces wide fluctuations when the calculation is done monthly

because you are comparing revenue against when supplies are purchased, not when they are consumed. Looking at this ratio on an annual basis is more meaningful, but you still have the same problem that exists with the staff expense ratio; unless someone is stealing supplies, the effect on this ratio from a "skimming" theft will be hard to spot.

3. Some ratios suffer from a weak causation link between the numerator and denominator. One ratio that many practices watch closely is the collection ratio. This ratio is collections divided by production. Some people calculate based on gross production, and I have seen other calculations where adjusted production is used as the base.

When calculated on an annual basis and one year is compared to the next, these ratios can illuminate some trends and issues. However, when people try to compare one month to the next, a problem becomes evident. What an insurance-based practice collects this month is largely dependent on last month's production. In a month when the doctor takes a vacation, the collection ratio looks amazing because the money collected from the previous full month's activity is being compared with revenue from a vacation-shortened month.

The following month's collection ratio looks miserable because now the phenomenon is reversed, and you are comparing diminished collections against a full month's production.

Looking at these ratios on an annual basis instead of monthly addresses this problem, but the impact of embezzlement on collection ratios is very small. If this is a rare situation where theft is limited to expense-side embezzlement such as payroll theft or stealing supplies with no skimming taking place, the impact on this collection ratio is nothing.

14

Why Did My Accountant Not Find the Embezzlement?

Most dentists expect their CPA to be their front line of embezzlement protection. And yet, the 2019 ADA study I have mentioned a couple of times determined that external accountants discovered only about 11% of embezzlement in dental offices.[46] While this percentage is higher than in most other industries (the ACFE says that nationwide, accountants detected about 3% of embezzlement),[47] it still represents a small percentage of detection. It is safe to conclude that most dentists overestimate the embezzlement protection provided by their annual accounting relationship.

---

[46] American Dental Association. (2019). 2018 CDP Survey on Employee Theft in the Dental Practice. *Center for Dental Practice*

[47] "Report to the Nations on Occupational Fraud and Abuse." *Association of Certified Fraud Examiners*, 2014, www.acfe.com/rttn-summary.aspx.

Before you conclude that CPAs are letting the dental community down (and as I am a CPA, I feel some obligation to defend the accounting profession), let me explain some of the elements of the relationship between a dentist and their CPA that you might not have considered.

First, accountants typically have a highly defined seasonal pattern to their workflow. A typical small accounting firm produces 40% of its annual revenue in three months,[48] and working 80-hour weeks is the norm for many accountants during tax season. Coincidentally, most dentists interact with their accountants at their CPA's busiest time of year. Interaction during a period of heavy workload limits the amount of mental energy and proactivity that your accountant can offer you.

Second, CPAs can perform three different levels of scrutiny and analysis when doing your work.[49]

1. An audit provides the highest level of assurance. When conducting an audit, your CPA will do sufficient analysis and independent verification to obtain "reasonable assurance that the financial statements are free from

---

[48]   Mendlowitz, Edward. "Art of Accounting: Easing Tax Season Workload Compression." *Accounting Today*, Accounting Today, 13 Nov. 2017, www.accountingtoday.com/opinion/art-of-accounting-easing-tax-season-workload-compression.

[49]   "Guide to Financial Statement Services: Compilation, Review and Audit." *AICPA*, www.aicpa.org/content/dam/aicpa/interestareas/privatecompaniespracticesection/qualityservicesdelivery/keepingup/downloadabledocuments/financial-statement-services-guide.pdf.

material misstatement."[50] An audit's primary focus is financial statement integrity, not embezzlement, and while an audit increases the chance of embezzlement detection, this is not the primary focus of an audit. Even so, audits can be prohibitively expensive ($25,000 to produce audited financial statements for a solo dental practice would not be out of the question), and for that reason, most dental practice owners, unless forced by a third party, like a bank, elect for lower levels of scrutiny, referred to as "review" or "compilation" engagements, and not a full "audit."

2. In the category of work immediately below an audit, called a review engagement, the accountant typically performs ratio analysis to obtain "limited assurance" that your statements do not need modifications.[51] This limited assurance does not extend to specifically to looking for embezzlement. Normally, some ratios are produced, and comparisons are made to results from previous years. As discussed in Chapter 13, because embezzlement normally consumes a small percentage of revenue, ratio analysis is unlikely to spot it.

---

[50] "Audit Risk and Materiality in Conducting an Audit." *Public Company Accounting Oversight Board*, pcaobus.org/Standards/Archived/Pages/AU312.aspx.

[51] "Guide to Financial Statement Services: Compilation, Review and Audit." *AICPA*, www.aicpa.org/content/dam/aicpa/interestareas/privatecompaniespracticesection/qualityservicesdelivery/keepingup/downloadabledocuments/financial-statement-services-guide.pdf.

3. The lowest category of accountant involvement is a compilation, which accountants sometimes refer to as a "write-up" engagement. In a compilation engagement, which is the least expensive, and not coincidentally also the most common relationship for dental practices, the CPA turns raw information, provided by you, into financial statements, without any scrutiny or analysis. It truly is a "garbage in – garbage out" arrangement.

It is not that the accountants are asleep at the switch; most dentists are not prepared to pay for any scrutiny of their information from their accountants. Even if they were prepared to pay for an enhanced mandate, there are some further limitations you should consider in terms of the accountant's knowledge level about embezzlement and the "window" through which the accountant can view your practice.

Prosperident has the privilege of working with some excellent CPA firms, and I am quick to defend the accounting profession against the sometimes unrealistic expectations of its clients. The lesson here is to ensure that you and your accountant are on the same page; accountants are happy to accept a mandate to provide higher assurance about your financial statements, but you have to grant that mandate and be prepared to pay for it.

Cash versus Accrual Accounting

There is another factor that most dentists do not consider. Most US dental practices can use the "cash basis of accounting" for income tax purposes.[52] Larger businesses must use "accrual" accounting, which measures revenue based on when work is billed to patients instead of when money is collected. Accrual accounting provides results that are closer to the true economic progress of a practice but is also more complicated and labor-intensive for accountants. "Cash basis" accounting is a simplification that is permitted for small businesses and allows income to be measured based on when money is received.

The difference between cash basis and accrual accounting is simply timing. Consider a start-up practice that, at the end of its first year, has $40,000 in receivables. If you are using cash accounting, the $40,000 is not considered part of that first year's income. Assuming that the entire amount is collected in the second year, it is part of the second year's income, but the receivables at the end of the second year are not included in Year 2's income.

Under the same scenario but using accrual accounting, the $40,000 (minus an estimate of uncollectability) is income in year 1 and is excluded from Year 2, but the receivables at the end of Year 2 are included in Year 2's income. Another way to look at this is that the accrual income for Year 2 is cash collections, minus opening receivables (because they have already been taxed in Year 1), plus receivables at the end of Year 2.

Income differences between the two methods are purely timing; over the entire life of a practice, cash and accrual accounting will yield the same taxable income. Cash accounting

---

52   McCool, Cameron. "Cash Basis Accounting vs. Accrual Accounting: Bench Accounting." *Bench*, 14 Feb. 2018, bench.co/blog/accounting/cash-vs-accrual-accounting/.

normally lowers income (and tax) in the early years of a practice and any other time when receivables are growing. Conversely, when receivables are shrinking (for example, in a practice's final year), cash-based accounting will result in higher taxable income than accrual accounting.

For a stable practice, normally, the difference between the opening and ending receivables is usually small, and the real benefit of cash accounting is a simplification; cash-based accounting really treats receivables as not existing, so they do not need to be balanced as part of the accounting function or need to be evaluated for collectability.

The downside of using the cash basis of accounting is that it permits "lazy accounting," where an accountant can completely ignore a dentist's practice management software and accounts receivable and perform their work from your practice's bank statements only. The ability to ignore receivables (and accounts payable too, for that matter) simplifies the accountant's work considerably. Still, it may mean that any unusual attributes of your receivables, which might be identified if you were using accrual accounting, will not be spotted.

While it is not strictly necessary in a practice using cash-basis accounting, some accountants will take the extra step of looking at summary reports from your practice management software. However, I have never seen an accountant look at individual transactions in a client's software, as doing so normally would be beyond their scope and expertise. This limitation restricts the possible embezzlement types that could be spotted by your accountant to relatively few methodologies.

Disconnect Between Accounting and Practice Management Software

Picture this conversation between a newly graduated dentist and her uncle, a CPA. The dentist is planning on opening a new practice. The accountant, being an accountant, asks the dentist how she plans to keep financial records.

The dentist proudly outlines that she has lined up a state-of-the-art practice management software to track revenue and that she will be using QuickBooks to keep track of her expenses.

The accountant asks the dentist how the two pieces of software will talk to each other, and the dentist realizes that, in fact, they won't.

The accountant's response is that this approach is dumb and will never work. He has a point, and yet this situation describes virtually every dental practice. Very few businesses track revenue and expenses using separate softwares. Because most practices use the cash method of accounting described earlier in this chapter, there is no forced convergence between these two pieces of software. And this leaves a gap that you can drive a truck through.

TWO INDEPENDENT PROCESSES

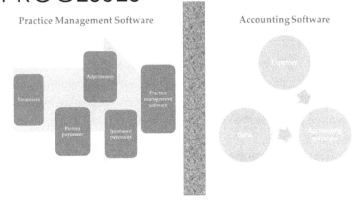

Figure 3 – Lack of overlap between practice management and accounting software

What is the Tax Status of Embezzled Funds?

Many dentists are a bit fuzzy on whether an embezzlement victim is forced to suffer the further indignity of paying tax on the money they stole.

If you are using the cash method of accounting, discussed earlier in this chapter, it's simple – there are very few ways that embezzled funds, no matter how stolen, can end up being taxed when you are using the cash method.

The only possibility I can think of would be if an employee overpaid themselves but somehow included the stolen money in the practice owner's own W2 form. Pulling all of this off would require access beyond what most dental staff have, so I think this possibility is remote.

If a practice uses accrual accounting, the question becomes more complicated, and it depends on at what point on its journey through the practice the money is stolen. This issue is something that we can help you navigate if you are an accrual-based practice.

I have Embezzlement Concerns. Should my Accountant Investigate?

For many dentists who have embezzlement concerns, their first call is to their CPA. While the accountant's perspective can be valuable, there may be some considerations of which the dentist should be aware.

Many of us fall into the trap of considering someone who knows 20% more about a subject than we do as an "expert." However, just as dentistry divides itself into general dentists and defined specialties, so does the accounting profession.

Many dentists deal with "generalist" CPAs who do not confine themselves to dealing with dentists or embezzlement investigation. While the generalists can do a decent job of converting your practice records into information that is usable by your bank and the IRS, they rarely have sufficient data to be able to benchmark your practice against others like a "Dental CPA," typically with 50 or more dental clients, can.

Even if you are using a CPA who specializes in working with dentists, it is highly unlikely that they have any specific training in embezzlement investigation. The "gold standard" in North

America for fraud investigation is the Certified Fraud Examiner (CFE) designation, which relatively few CPAs, and even fewer dental CPAs, possess.

To properly assist you with an embezzlement concern in your practice, you need to find someone who possesses several distinct competencies:

1. They need to understand how a dental office works, dental terminology, coding, etc.
2. They must have significant expertise in working with practice management software, preferably the practice management software you are using. This experience requirement goes well beyond looking at reports that you printed for them; they need to have worked in the software as a user and, at a minimum, should be able to find a specific transaction and generate a custom report. The needed level of expertise is far beyond what most CPAs can bring.
3. If you are a specialist, particularly one who uses practice management software designed specifically for your specialty, experience working within that specialty and software is important. In particular, orthodontists and oral surgeons, because of the nature of their workflow and software, need hyper-specialized investigators.
4. An effective investigator also must have training in embezzlement investigation and preferably considerable experience in performing investigation in dental practices. Because of the methodologies used in dental embezzlement, experience at investigating

internal theft at a pharmacy or building supply company is not of much value when looking at dental office embezzlement.

It is entirely possible that your bright, knowledgeable, and otherwise well-qualified accountant cannot provide the kind of assistance that you need for this problem. Unfortunately, I have seen many "well-intentioned dabblers" who are not fully aware of the knowledge and experience required to complete this kind of work successfully and rush in where they should not.

Most accountants also are not well equipped to think like criminals. For most of what they do, this is hardly a character flaw. However, it reduces their ability to spot embezzlement.

Before Prosperident hires someone as an investigator, we usually require them to have at least a decade of working in the dental field before commencing their training with us. Many of our team are Certified Fraud Examiners. About a third of them are former practicing dentists. We have separate departments for areas requiring narrow expertise like orthodontics and oral surgery. All our investigators live and breathe dental embezzlement daily and are incredibly well trained.

15

Theft in Orthodontic Practices

People are often surprised when I tell them that our team includes investigators who specialize in investigating embezzlement in orthodontic practices.

We do this because the business model of orthodontic practices, and the practice management software used, are very different from general dental practices. Where general dental (and specialties including pediatric, endodontic, periodontic, prosthodontic and to a lesser extent oral and maxillofacial surgery practices) all require their software to perform a similar task of billing insurance companies and determining remaining balances owed by patients, orthodontic practice management software really monitors "contracts" or payment arrangements between paying parties and the practice. These contracts may extend over several years, and the interaction between insurance and the portion paid by patients is, to say the least, unusual.

For this reason, the embezzlement patterns seen in orthodontic practices can take radically different forms than what happens in general dental practice or those of other specialties.

Back in the "dark ages" 20 years ago, our investigators (who at that time were non-specialized and therefore covered all branches of dentistry) used to cringe mightily when we told them that we had an orthodontic case for them to investigate. After watching enough of those pained expressions, we made the decision to hire a specialized capability to investigate orthodontic practices.

One type of practice that is rapidly growing in prevalence is the combined orthodontic-pediatric practice. Until recently, there was a dearth of software designed to handle both kinds of practice simultaneously. While we have been pleased to see the emergence of software designed for this specific situation, many of these practices continue to use two pieces of practice management software, with one being used for ortho treatments and the second when patients receive pediatric dentistry. This split software makes for some administrative awkwardness for practice staff. For example, when patients have a balance in each system, it makes for a challenging embezzlement investigation for us. Fortunately, Wendy Askins, who heads our ortho department, has proven herself capable of handling this problem's complications.

If you are an orthodontist with embezzlement issues, please recognize the specialized nature of your situation and that neither a generalized fraud investigator nor an investigator familiar with investigation in general dental practices can provide the help you need. Your specialty requires comparable specialization in your investigator.

16

Handling of Funds and Balancing by Staff

As discussed in Chapter 12, there are two ways that a thief can steal from a dental practice. If he or she believes that the practice owner does not do "oversight," or if such oversight is only partially done, stealing is uncomplicated. If, as a thief, I can arrange for the bank deposit to be less than what the practice management software indicates that it should be, then "shorting" the deposit is how I will steal. This theft pattern, which we call "reconciliation theft," is a crude way to steal, in the sense that the evidence of stealing is completely visible if only someone bothers to look. Because it is so simple and does not require any action to be taken in your practice management software, reconciliation theft is within the grasp of even the dumbest, laziest thief imaginable.

What this thief is counting on, based on their observation of your patterns, is that you will not be looking.

If a thief believes that you are doing a thorough oversight, they can still steal, but it requires a more sophisticated approach. We call this "concealment theft," and at its core is the thief figuring out how to make practice management software lie about the amount of funds collected.

For purposes of this discussion, we refer to "balancing" as the day-end process carried out by staff and "oversight" or "reconciliation" as the supervisory process that should be done by the practice owner or someone delegated by the owner to perform the internal audit function. Both balancing and oversight are necessary for an office's financial information to have integrity. The purpose of balancing is to find errors and omissions and to create front-desk accountability. Balancing is not likely to find embezzlement (because frequently the person stealing is the same person performing the balancing) but must be done for the practice owner to reconcile.

Daily Balancing is not Foolproof

Balancing is at the core of every practice management software system, and for that matter, the manual "pegboard" system that preceded computerization. Daily balancing in a computerized practice involves printing the day-end report for the software (often referred to as a "day sheet", although it has different names in different practice management softwares) and making a comparison between the "collections" reported on this day sheet and the funds deposited by the practice.

Many dentists believe that, if their day sheet collections balance to the bank deposit every day, they are completely safe from being embezzled.

It continues to amaze me the number of dentists who do not know the first thing about their practice management software. That software is as essential to the success of your practice as your handpiece or your imaging equipment. Yet, every week, I encounter dentists who cannot even log in to their own software or perform some elementary functions.

Let me be emphatic about this. Practice management software is not going to go away, and every practice owner needs to recognize this and develop a basic level of competence in their software.

Shockingly, there are also many offices where the oversight activity never happens, and the finances of the practice are completely left in the hands of staff. There are a couple of big concerns with this. First, if balancing is not supervised, it is possible that balancing is not being done at all or that it is done incorrectly. Among other things, balancing is a key check against clerical errors.

Second, and more important, as discussed, a lack of oversight allows reconciliation theft, the easiest pathway to embezzlement, to take place. Suppose you are not checking the deposit against practice management software, as discussed in Chapter 12. As mentioned, you have left the door open for a thief to steal without any need to try to conceal the theft in your practice management software.

There are many practices where oversight is partially completed. It is very common, for example, for a practice owner to check the "physical" deposit, which could include cash and checks (or cash only, if a check scanner is used) yet ignore the "electronic deposit," including credit card payments and other amounts that appear electronically. If a partial oversight is done, a thief will quickly orient their stealing to the part of the deposit that is not reconciled.

However, even if every day's collections and deposit balances perfectly, this does not mean that you are safe from embezzlement. Dentists tend to believe that the day sheet is "right" because it comes from their computer, is nicely formatted, and is produced by sophisticated practice management software. It is human nature to accept the veracity of documents that arrive on this basis. However, what these dentists are forgetting is that most or all transactions in the software are entered by staff. It is not difficult for a staff member to make the day sheet say whatever they want it to, making it balance to a bank deposit reduced by embezzlement. Thieves are both motivated and clever and generally have little trouble finding a way to make the day sheet present an untrue picture.

Put slightly differently; if your bank deposit does not balance to your day sheet, you probably have an embezzlement issue. However, the reverse is not true — the fact that these things balance may mean nothing more than that your embezzler knows how to add.

Please do not take us out of context — carefully checking the day sheet is something every dentist needs to do daily. Failure to perform oversight to check the daily balancing, delegating oversight to a staff member, or doing it improperly just makes it much easier for a thief to steal. If you are reconciling correctly (we will discuss how to do this in Chapter 17), you can still be stolen from, but it becomes more difficult, and the probability that you will detect it increases dramatically.

In addition to blocking the easiest avenue to embezzlement, a doctor's day sheet review serves one other important purpose. It gives you a good chance to catch clerical errors or treatment that, for some reason, was performed but did not get entered into the practice management software. While this isn't embezzlement, the cost of these errors can be considerable.

An Oversight Story

I remember early in my career being called by a dentist with embezzlement concerns. He didn't have any staff members behaving like they were stealing, but he certainly had a profitability issue, which he thought might be a result of embezzlement.

One of the first things I did when I was retained was to look at some day sheets. I quickly realized that there was no radiography whatsoever being billed from the hygienists' operatories. I asked the doctor whether hygienists took their own x-rays or if this was always done in the dentist's chair. I also asked if imaging was always entered with the dentist instead of the hygienist in his practice management software, even if a hygienist took the x-ray. He replied that the hygienists were very regular about having current radiographs for the doctor when he arrived to examine patients. Hygienists took their own films and radiography would properly be coded to the hygienists.

After a bit of digging, I realized what was happening. The hygienists would place the x-rays that they had taken into the patient charts (this was back in the days of celluloid film and paper charts, and before there were terminals in operatories).

The hygienists assumed that when the charts got to the front desk, the receptionist checking the patients out would see film in the charts and enter the correct imaging code into practice management software, so the hygienists view charting the x-rays as redundant and a waste of their time. Of course, the receptionists did not have the ability or mandate to chart for the hygienists and did not pick up on the missed charges, so patients were walking away without being charged for the imaging work that had been done.

When you consider the missed revenue on 20-30 patients per day in this practice, the money falling through the cracks from this simple disconnect was about $80,000 per year, which certainly was a big part of the productivity issue. I gave the dentist a bit of a scolding because the missing x-ray fees were certainly something that he would have noticed if he had only bothered to look at his practice's day sheets.

It has Become More Complicated to Balance

I should also mention that the task of determining whether your software truly balances against your deposit is considerably more complicated than it once was. When I started working with dentists in 1989, check scanners and merchant terminals did not exist, insurance companies making automated deposits to a practice's bank account were unheard of, there were no entities like CareCredit or Lending Club that made direct deposits to your account, and when someone paid by credit card, their credit card information was imprinted on a paper form, which the practice would deposit to the bank just like a check. In those days, the **entire** deposit was physically carried to the bank, and it was relatively easy to see whether the deposit agreed with the (manual pegboard) records of the practice. Embezzlement still took place, of course, but the reconciliation theft that we see so much of now was uncommon.

Fast forward to today. Now, deposited funds may arrive at the bank in many ways (carried to the bank, deposited by scanning checks with a check scanner, directly deposited by an insurance company or a patient financing company, deposited directly via your "merchant terminal" that accepts credit card payments, etc.). Some of these deposits inherently create "timing differences" when funds arrive in your bank earlier or later than when they are recorded in your practice management software.

For example, if a patient pays by credit card today, this is recorded as being received in your practice management software today. However, the credit card company's processing typically takes time, so this payment will not be deposited into your bank for a couple of business days. Conversely, when an insurance company makes an electronic deposit to your account (the correct terms for these is Automated Clearing House or "ACH" deposits), the funds will usually be in your bank before your practice receives the Explanation of Benefits ("EOB") from the insurance company. I'll discuss the complications that ACH deposits create later in this chapter.

The problem that these timing differences create is that it is impossible to do real-time oversight anymore. If you are comparing the deposit being made with the day sheet from your software at the end of a day, you cannot possibly know yet whether the correct amount will show up in your bank account from credit card payments. Equally, unless you have online access to your bank account and check it, you are also taking it on faith that the amount shown on your day sheet for ACH deposits (which some day sheets refer to as "bulk payments") is identical to what was deposited in your bank. Oversight has become a lot more complicated than it once was, and in most dental practices, the systems in use have not adapted to the more complex environment.

Electronic Funds Transfers

Both insurance companies and dental practices have long appreciated the convenience of electronic funds transfers (sometimes referred to as "direct deposit" or "automated clearing house" payments) as a method of payment. From the insurance company's perspective, EFTs provide an economical way to discharge their obligations to dentists that avoids the manual elements of printing and mailing checks to practices. For practice owners, being paid more quickly and the convenience of not having to carry the funds to the bank were appealing.

Many advisors to dentists have also espoused electronic funds transfers as a way of lowering a practice's risk for embezzlement. Their logic is that a direct transfer of funds from an insurance company to your bank keeps money out of the reach of a would-be embezzler and therefore prevents that money from being embezzled.

In Chapter 20, we discuss division of duties between team members. While making use of electronic funds transfers does remove the "receive funds" duty from staff at least for the EFTs, the complications it creates for the balancing process more than outweigh any benefit achieved from that division.

While there was a time when I thought EFTs were a good idea, I have recently had a change of heart on the wisdom of being paid by electronic funds transfer and I **no longer recommend that practices be paid by EFT.**

The Problem with Electronic Funds Transfers

Not recommending EFTs is a bold statement, and it is bucking a lot of conventional wisdom. Here is the reasoning:

While I won't go into details, it is not hard for an enterprising thief to instruct an insurance company to redirect EFTs to their own account. We recently worked on a case where EFT payments were still going into a thief's account six months after the thief was fired by the practice.

As an embezzler, I am not trying to steal 100% or 60% of your incoming funds. My happy place is normally 2-4% of your collections.

Even if 100% of your insurance proceeds arrive via EFT, there is plenty left for me to steal. Every practice collects co-payments from patients, and these payments will arrive by cash, check or credit card. I can easily achieve my target theft from these "over the counter" payments.

With most practices having check scanners, the "we save a trip to the bank" logic, which at one point was a major benefit from EFT payments, no longer applies.

The big downside to receiving payments by EFT is that doing so removes one of the basic safeguards that practices rely on to ensure accuracy of posting — daily balancing. When cash, checks or credit cards are posted to patient accounts, many posting errors are found because, when the office manager performs balancing at the end of that day, the collections according to practice management software do not equal the deposit being made to the bank. Because normally practice staff don't (and shouldn't) have access to a practice's bank account, there is really nothing to balance EFT postings against. So, a math error will probably not be picked up because the out of balance condition it creates will normally not be visible to the person doing the balancing.

Second, the trigger for posting an electronic funds transfer payment is an Explanation of Benefits (EOB) sent to the practice. If an EOB never arrives at the practice or gets lost by the practice, there is no "flag" to alert the practice staff that funds have been deposited in the practice's account (in other words that the patient's balance has been paid) but no posting has been made in practice management software. In comparison, if an office is performing day-end balancing (which every practice should) it is impossible to deposit a check without posting a payment to a patient's account.

Third, EFTs create a "timing difference." As discussed earlier in this chapter, timing differences occur when money arrives at your bank at a different time from when it is posted to practice management software. Timing differences make the process of overseeing the balancing activities of your office manager much more challenging, because they require you to maintain a "watch list" of deferred amounts and to confirm that these amounts do show up. With EFTs, insurance companies normally initiate the funds transfer and produce the corresponding EOB simultaneously. The funds transfer is virtually instantaneous. The EOB must arrive at the practice, and then be processed by a human, normally resulting in a multi-day delay.

This timing difference is made worse because in many practices, staff feel no urgency to post EOBs from electronic funds transfers (under the logic that "the doctor already has her money") which exacerbates the timing difference between receipt of funds and posting in practice management software. In a busy office, the result may be a lag of days or weeks until staff find time to post EOBs for electronic transfers. In contrast, assuming that day-end balancing is being performed and daily deposits are made, it is impossible to experience a timing difference with a check payment. We will discuss how a practice owner can work through timing differences to effect a reconciliation in Chapter 17.

Electronic Funds Transfers Often Manipulated in Embezzlement

In the course of our work, we have seen many embezzlements perpetuated through EFT manipulation. Beyond that, we also see where accepting electronic funds transfers is a significant contributor to financial disorganization in many practices. For these reasons, our recommendation is that practices discontinue accepting EFTs from insurance companies and require those companies to pay by check.

Balancing

Here are some of the things that should happen when balancing is being done by staff:

Producer Review

I love the approach taken by a friend of mine, Sandy Baird, a practice management consultant based in Tennessee. Sandy says that the day-end routine needs to be a team concept and that team members other than the practice owner also have roles. For example, Sandy suggests that each associated dentist, assistant, and hygienist needs to print a production report for their own activities, compare it with their schedule and ensure that correct fees and procedures were applied, that work performed was coded to the correct provider, and to indicate this by signing off on their individual production report. This verification is not a substitute for the owner's review of the practice but increases the chances of finding inaccuracies.

Here are some of the things that Sandy expects producers to look at:

1. Are all the procedures and procedure codes performed listed? For instance, as was the case with my friend's practice discussed earlier in the chapter, it is common to

omit radiographs. Omitted procedures, no matter how small, can grow to large sums of money if frequently missed. Such omissions could be accidental, or they could be a sign of an embezzler's work.

2. Are the correct teeth numbers, surfaces, and patient names correct? Errors like these can be a nightmare to straighten out with insurance. If the front desk knows that day about such an error, they can change it before submitting their bulk claims.

3. Are the procedures attributed to the correct provider? If not, producer fees, reports, goals, and bonus calculations may be inaccurate, not to mention insurance. Incorrect provider attribution is a favorite playground of embezzlers, as well.

4. Does each procedure have an appropriate fee connected to it? Perhaps a fee has been omitted or deleted accidentally or on purpose.

5. After completing these steps, they are to write any errors they catch and changes necessary on their report, sign or initial it, and submit it to the front desk to make necessary changes before the insurance is submitted and the end of the day processes are completed. These sheets will be included in the practice owner's end of the day packet put on their desk each evening.

Office Manager's Responsibilities

After all patients' procedures are completed, and all that day's payments entered, your office manager's job is to:

1. Balance the practice management software's total for cash against the amount of cash on hand for deposit. Please see Chapter 20 for a discussion of how to handle cash on hand.
2. Balance the practice management software's total for checks against checks to be deposited.
3. Balance payments from the practice management software's total for credit card payments to the merchant terminal's daily batch total.
4. Reconcile any third-party financing (e.g., CareCredit) from practice management software against a daily report for that entity.
5. Balance the total of ACH deposits for the day according to the practice management software against EOBs processed during the day.
6. Once balancing is complete, sign the day sheet.
7. Steps 1 to 5 should be checked by a second employee who also signs the report.
8. Create the Practice owner's End of the Day Packet, which contains the following.
   a. The deposit and deposit slip for bank drop, if the owner is taking the deposit to the bank.
   b. All the clinical end of the day reviewed production reports discussed above.
   c. A printed copy of the software's daily deposit slip report, and, yes, a daily deposit is required.
      While making a deposit every day used to be de rigueur for practices, particularly for practice that use scanners to deposit checks, it

may not make sense to go to the bank every day to deposit the small amount of cash coming in.

It is fine to make deposits less frequently, for example, once a week. However, each day's cash should be made as a separate deposit. If bank deposits are made on Fridays, four or five deposits should be made one after the other, depending on how many days were worked that week.

If you are not using a check scanner and are taking the checks to the bank, when deposit slips are prepared, do not allow the staff member creating the deposit slip to list checks received as a total amount only. Each individual check needs to be itemized on the deposit slip. Although this is tedious, if this is done, sorting out irregularities later becomes a huge challenge.

Having a team member take the bank deposit is acceptable as long as the practice owner is diligent about conducting oversight. In other words, it is far less important that you take money to the bank yourself than that you have a mechanism to ensure that the correct amount was deposited.

d. The day-end report from the "merchant terminal" that accepts credit card payments for the practice.

e. This Practice Owner's Packet is given to the practice owner at the end of each day.

You may hear comments from your team like, "Oh, doctor, what a waste of paper. There is no need to print these documents." The answer is, yes, there is a very real reason to print these documents. Hard copies freeze the day in time. Digital documents are easily manipulated and changed with few clues to show they have been altered. To know what you were truly given and saw on any day, you must print it.

Wendy Askins, a Supervising Examiner at Prosperident, makes a very good point about "payment codes" in management software not being used properly. These codes are used to categorize payments as they come in.

There is only one purpose for these codes – to facilitate balancing and oversight. Some practices use insufficient codes to do this. For example, we see practices that classify payments as "patient payment" or "insurance payment" only. This minimalist approach makes it impossible to, for example, determine if the amount paid by credit cards today agrees with the practice management software. In other offices, there are excessive codes (for example, having a separate code for each insurance company's checks). Using excessive codes means that you will have to add several totals from the practice management software to balance against the total checks deposited.

The rule here is simple – we need a separate code for cash, checks, and each activity that produces a separate line item on your monthly banking statement. For example, if your merchant account deposits Visa and MasterCard together as one line item but American Express separately, you need one code for Visa/MC and a separate one for AMEX.

17

Financial Oversight of Your Practice

In Chapter 16, we discussed how your staff should handle and account for funds received by your practice. Now let's discuss your role. And the next statement is probably the most important one in this entire book.

Every employee of your practice who handles funds needs supervision.

If you have an office with three receptionists and an office manager, it is the job of the office manager to supervise the financial activities of the receptionists. Few readers would take issue with that statement.

However, it is the next statement that is often in contrast with what happens in practices – **it is the job of the practice owner to exercise financial supervision of the office manager.**

In many, many of the embezzlement cases we see, practice owners are startlingly uninvolved in the financial operations of their practices. Chapter 4 discusses what prompts embezzlers to steal, and uninvolved practice owners are really playing Russian Roulette. Sooner or later the right set of conditions will exist that causes someone in your employ to want to steal. If unsupervised they can get away with it for an extended period and steal a staggering amount of money.

If your desire as a dentist is to be a "pure clinician" and not to involve yourself in the business component of dentistry, that is a completely legitimate desire. However, you should recognize that achieving that goal is fundamentally incompatible with practice ownership. The good news is that there are plenty of practice situations available to you – become a military dentist, teach at university (although please don't become the instructor for a practice management course), become a public health dentist, work for Indian Health Services, be an associate, or affiliate with a DSO.

If you want to own a dental practice and enjoy the numerous financial and lifestyle advantages of practice ownership, you must concurrently accept the responsibilities of being an owner. And one of the biggest responsibilities is oversight.

What Comprises Oversight?

Financial oversight consists of daily, monthly, and annual activities. The oversight plan for your practice will reflect a lot of factors including the knowledge, skill, and trustworthiness of your team as well as your own capabilities and the availability of outside advisors to whom some activities can be outsourced. Here are the core activities of oversight:

General Principles:

There are three objectives to your oversight. The first is to ensure that your practice management software correctly captures what happened. If this is not the case, any further oversight activities will be useless because they are based on flawed information. Ensuring accuracy is accomplished by conducting a **daily review,** discussed later in this chapter.

The second principle is to ensure that the daily reporting that you have reviewed has captured **everything** that was entered this month into your practice management software. In other words, you want to be sure that no transactions managed to do an end-run around the reporting that you have scrutinized in detail. Verifying that nothing has snuck by your scrutiny is accomplished by an **articulation verification**, which will also be discussed in this chapter.

And finally, having validated the initial entry of transactions into your practice management software and that there are no transactions that bypassed the daily reporting that you have scrutinized, you are now able to verify that the amount collected according to practice management software agrees with the amount deposited in your bank account. Traditionally, this activity was performed at the end of each day. However, as the complexity of financial flows to practices has increased, trying to match deposits to collections has become more challenging, and performing a **monthly reconciliation** is both more efficient and more rigorous.

The Daily Review

Every practice management software has a daily report designed for the end of day review. It may be called a "daily summary," "day-end report," or "day sheet," or it may have a different name in your software. For purposes of this discussion, I will refer to it as the "day sheet."

Day sheets can be produced to cover the entire practice or limited to the activities of a specific provider. As a practice owner, you will want the "whole practice" report, and I also suggest printing one for each provider, the use of which will be discussed below.

The day sheet will normally show procedures performed, fees associated with those procedures, payments received, and adjustments made, as well as any deletions or corrections that were made. Normally at the bottom of the report are totals for each of these activities, plus a breakdown of the payments received by type (cash, check, credit card payment, third party deposit, etc.)

Some day sheets also show your accounts receivable balance at the beginning of the day and the balance at the end of the day. If the day sheet from your practice management software is missing some of this information, you will need to print additional reports to ensure that you have everything listed in this paragraph.

Other reports from your practice management software will isolate any one of these items into a single report. For example, most software will generate an adjustments report that only lists adjustments or a production report that isolates procedures performed, and fees billed. These reports have their uses and allow you to review a specific type of transaction. However, for the day-end review that you are performing, you are best served by a report that allows you to see all the activities undertaken for each patient today in a single report.

For a patient who visited the practice for treatment, you can see what was billed, what was paid, and any adjustments or modifications that were made. This review is preferable to, for example, looking at today's adjustments in a separate report, which means that you will not have the context for the adjustments made. Put another way, a $200 adjustment on $1,600 of treatment means something quite different from the same $200 adjustment applied to a $250 treatment, and looking at an adjustment report simply will not give you that context without cross-referencing to other reports. The day sheet, if generated with the proper settings, will allow you to have all the information needed for your daily review in a single report.

One more important consideration - the day sheet and other reports from your practice management software used in this process need to be printed by you, your spouse, or an external person like a bookkeeper or accountant. You should never rely on a staff member to generate the reports used for oversight. The person printing a report has considerable control over the parameters used to generate that report. Accordingly, allowing staff members to print and hand you reports opens the possibility of "selective reporting" where certain activities are excluded from the reports you are given. When selective reporting is done, you may think that the report you are using summarizes the entire practice when it does not.

I suggest limiting your daily review of reports to the single purpose of ensuring accuracy of entry of transactions. For the reasons I will outline below, I would not try to perform the reconciliation of collections to deposits daily. Doing this financial reconciliation monthly is far more efficient and keeps the day-end activity to five minutes or less. The daily objective is to make sure that transactions entered into practice management software accurately reflect what happened. It is the easiest thing for what was really a three-surface filling to get entered into software as a two-surface restoration. There may or may not be embezzlement involved, but at a minimum, this error represents lost revenue to your practice.

Normally the best way to conduct this review is for each member of your team who is a "biller" (dentist, hygienist, dental assistant performing assisted hygiene, etc.) to review a report isolating their own work for accurate entry, and it is an excellent idea to require them to sign the day-end report that covers their work. As the practice owner, you review what happened in your operatories, plus look at a "whole practice" report as a double-check on your team.

A delayed review of a day is close to useless. Your ability to find an error or unusual transaction degrades considerably with even a 24-hour delay in performing the review. Looking at last Thursday's report on Monday afternoon represents a lost opportunity to find inaccuracies.

When reviewing the day-end report, there are several things you should scrutinize:

1. Review all fees that were billed for accuracy. Embezzlement is not the only threat to your practice's revenue; simple clerical mistakes can also be costly. A one-digit error in a procedure code can cost you hundreds of dollars.

2. Review payments received. One thing to check is to look at patients' payments during the day to ensure that your policies for collecting co-pays are being followed. In other words, if your policy is to collect co-payments (or at least estimates thereof) on walk-out, your day sheet will tell you whether team members are following this policy.

3. Ensure that there was a fee charged for every patient you saw today unless you know that a specific patient was booked for a "no-charge" appointment (an example of a no-charge appointment is a visit within a multi-visit procedure that had a single fee, such as an ortho check if your practice does orthodontic treatment).

4. Review all adjustments (both debit and credit adjustments) and ensure that you understand the reason for them and that the adjustments make sense in the context. Substituting an adjustment code for a payment code is one of the most basic methods of concealing theft. Also, you should require (and check for) proper categorization of adjustments. In contrast to payment types (where it is desirable only to have a few categories) for adjustments, we want sufficient categories to capture every distinct adjustment type. Whenever an adjustment does not fit into the categories

you have created, staff will use a "miscellaneous adjustment" category. This category is one to watch very carefully. You should require (and monitor) that a detailed explanation needs to be entered into the patient's record any time this category is used. Check the notes made to ensure that you agree with the basis for the adjustment and that it does not fit within one of the defined adjustment categories. And if there are a fair number of miscellaneous adjustments made for the same reason, this is a good time to place a label on that type of situation and create a tailored adjustment code for it. Whatever the cause of an adjustment, it represents money out of your pocket, and for that reason, it requires scrutiny comparable to if you were writing a check for the same amount.

5. When reviewing the work of hygienists, does the frequency of things like radiography and recall exams line up with your practice policies?

6. Ensure that all patients are "checked out" in your practice management software. Checking out is the process of closing an appointment in practice management software. Checking out a patient forces the front desk staff to either apply a charge or record a patient as having had a no-charge appointment. When any patient who had chargeable work done is not checked out, you have lost money.

Once reviews are completed and everyone has signed off, collect the individual reports, staple them to the practice-wide report, and put the package in a locked cabinet or drawer. You will need it again at the end of the month.

There is no particular benefit to having an external party review the day sheet or the daily balancing done by the office management software. As discussed, the point of your day-end review is to ensure accuracy of primary information entered into your practice management software, and only the people who did or assisted in the work are in the position to ensure accuracy.

Articulation

To a dentist, articulation refers to the way that a patient's mandible and maxilla should fit together. Similarly, your reports should fit together smoothly, and verifying this is an essential part of your month-end routine.

Remember those day sheets that you reviewed and put away? The month-end is the time to retrieve them. The other thing you need is a summary report from your practice management software (think of it as a "month sheet" if you like – I think I just invented that term, but it fits nicely) that provides monthly totals for fees, collections, and payments.

The goal of the articulation process is to ensure that the daily totals add up exactly to the totals for the month sheet. The easiest way to do this is to use a spreadsheet to enter the totals from each day sheet and then have the spreadsheet sum the fees, collections, and payments from the day sheets you saved. And here is the important part – the totals from your spreadsheet should exactly match the numbers on your month sheet. If the day sheets do not articulate with the month sheet, this normally means that someone posted some transactions outside business hours, presumably things they did not want you to see, and some further digging is warranted to see what has been hidden from you.

If you aren't good with spreadsheets, we are happy to supply you with a simple template that you can use each month. Email us at requests@prosperident.com and we will be happy to give it to you.

Monthly Reconciliation

When I first worked in dentistry, end-of-day balancing by staff and doctor oversight were virtually universal. In the 1980s and 1990s the flow of funds into a practice was much simpler than it is today, and reconciling daily made more sense than trying to do it monthly given the reporting that was produced by the old manual pegboard system, which really didn't have useful month-end reporting. It also reflected a dogged determination to catch a thief on the first day that they stole something. While I respect the sentiment, the difference between catching them on day 1 versus day 20 probably isn't material for most practices, so I am not sure that rationale continues to apply.

As technology like merchant terminals, check scanners and electronic funds transfers took hold in dental practices, daily balancing and the doctor's oversight thereof became increasingly challenging, to the point where many offices no longer even attempt to perform these functions. The problem is that a suitable replacement has never been implemented in these practices, and that having no oversight in this area leaves a practice owner vulnerable to some rudimentary theft.

Given how funds flow and banking is done currently, performing a reconciliation monthly instead of daily offers several advantages. First, it takes far less of the doctor's time to perform one larger reconciliation than to do 20 smaller ones.

Second, it allows the practice owner to work from statements from your bank, merchant service provider and third-party financing companies instead of deposit slips and other. Because these statements reach you directly from the issuing party, they are much more difficult for a thief to adulterate than daily records. These statements are also complete – they demonstrably cover the entire month.

We have seen many cases of doctors working from deposit slips to perform reconciliations get fooled by a staff member who altered the totals on the slips, and others who got taken by someone performing transactions on a merchant terminal after hours (and of course not proving the batch tape printed by the terminal to the practice owner).

And third, looking at a month at a time drastically reduces the relative magnitude of timing differences, which will be discussed more fully later in this chapter.

The process for performing monthly reconciliation is simple:

1. Determine monthly collections from the "month sheet" referred to in Chapter 16
2. Next grab your bank statement. Most bank statements total your deposits for the month at the bottom of the

statement. If you have multiple bank accounts, you will need to repeat the following steps for each account.

3. While it is tempting to work from this total deposit number, it may contain types of deposits that are not reflected in your practice management software, and you must first "normalize" by subtracting any credits to your account that are not "dental revenue" amounts. Examples include credits from transfers from other accounts, interest earned on deposits, tax refunds, loan advances, rebates, and any other deposits that don't relate to patient or insurance payments.

4. You also need to consider whether any deposits have had some kind of deduction from them. For example, while most credit card processing companies deposit full amounts paid by patients and debit your account for their fees once per month, maddeningly there are a few companies that deduct their free from each payment (i.e., a patient pays $100 and the deposit to your account is $97.50 or something). Some patient finance companies where the doctor financially participates in the cost of financing will also do this. If this kind of deduction is being made, your deposits will appear to be short by the amount of the deductions. The best thing you can do is to look for an alternate provider of these services that fully deposits and takes their fees once per month by debit from your bank account.

Let's refer to the deposit amount after allowing for these factors as the "adjusted deposit." Will the adjusted deposit equal the amount of collections from your month sheet? Not likely, and the probable culprit is timing differences.

Timing Differences

We introduced the concept of timing differences in Chapter 16, and they refer to situations where a transaction is recognized on a different day in practice management software than when the money appears in your bank account. Timing differences create challenges in validating collections against deposits, because a simple comparison of collections against adjusted deposits does not consider timing differences, and a result of an inability to deal with timing differences properly, many practices have stopped the vital activities of balancing and reconciliation. If stealing is taking place, timing differences may mask missing money.

There are a few things that can be done to make timing differences less of a factor in reconciliation:

1.   Opting out of electronic funds transfers and being paid by check by insurance companies can eliminate a major portion of your timing differences. When the check and Explanation of Benefits arrive simultaneously, they will be processed by your team on the same day. This means that you will have far fewer transactions that give rise to timing differences.
2.   By moving the validation period from the traditionally used single day to a month, you allow most timing differences to self-correct. As long as both the practice

management software entry and the bank deposit fall within the same month, they do not present as a timing difference when you look at the month as a whole; it is only transactions that overhang the first or last day of the month that must be dealt with as exceptions. Moving to a monthly reconciliation offers some other advantages. It is far less work to do one bigger reconciliation than 20 smaller ones. Also, it would be impractical and expensive to outsource daily reconciliations, but outsourcing a monthly one is far more feasible.

3. Ensure that your deposits are not "batched." In other words, if you only go to the bank once per week, you should make a separate deposit for each day for which you have a day sheet. So, if your practice is closed on Fridays, and you make deposits on Thursdays, there should be four deposits made each Thursday. This doesn't change the quantum or magnitude of timing differences, but it makes them much easier to isolate if needed.

Once you have compared practice management software collections against adjusted deposits, and if they don't quite line up, the challenge with the "variance" is how to differentiate between timing differences and missing money, which is a "permanent difference."

There are a few possible approaches. One solution is to look at transactions of the types that produce timing differences slightly before and after the beginning and end of the month and try to account for the difference. This can be labor-intensive and requires you to think more like an accountant than a dentist.

Another approach is to hand this problem to someone like an external bookkeeper to resolve. Most bookkeepers have a good eye for detail and should be able to resolve this for you. The downsides are that it will cost money, and many bookkeepers have limited familiarity with practice management software. It is ok to outsource reconciliation and chasing the transactions straddling the beginning and end of the month; it is not OK to have a staff member do this work.

The easiest solution is to take a slightly statistical approach to the problem. Timing differences reverse once the second part of the transaction takes place.

Let's say, for example, that in July a patient pays $4,000 by credit card on the last day of the month (which means that the money will not reach your bank account until August), and that this transaction is the only one for July that has a timing difference. When you compare collections against adjusted deposits for July, you will have collections greater than adjusted deposits by $4,000. However, you will be starting August with a $4,000 deposit and no offsetting entry in practice management software, because the practice management software entry already happened in July. So, if that was the only timing difference for August, you would end August with bank greater than practice management software by $4,000.

Over the months of July and August, the variances cancel each other out so that the aggregate variance is zero. Of course, this was done in a simplified example and is less visible with variances at both the beginning and end of both months, but we can use the concept that variances from timing differences eventually zero out to help us differentiate them from permanent differences. Setting it up initially is a bit technical but once set up, it makes the month-end activity much quicker. Here is how to do it:

1. As you determine each month's variance, enter it into a spreadsheet.
2. Total the cumulative variance from the past six months
3. Plot the cumulative variances into a "scatter plot." I'd suggest that you plot the last six months of data each month when you do this.
4. Spreadsheets have a function to fit a line to a series of points in a scatter plot. In Excel, this function is called "Fit Trendline." The underlying math to produce the trendline is linear regression, which you probably studied in a statistics course and promptly forgot.

If the trendline has a slope approximating zero, you can safely attribute the variances to timing. However, if the cumulative variance is increasing over time (in other words, that the trendline has a discernable slope), something other than timing differences is at play.

Please see the two examples below.

Figure 4 – Timing differences only

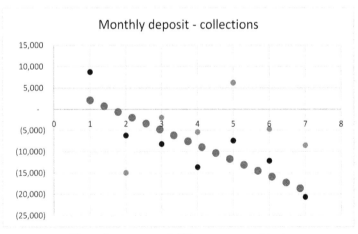

Figure 5 – permanent differences are evident.

The trendline in Figure 4 has a zero slope, which suggests that the cumulative monthly variance is not increasing, meaning that the variance is caused exclusively by timing differences. In Figure 5, however, the line has a noticeable slope, meaning that something other than timing differences is also at play.

As part of our Owner Proactive Strategies product, we offer comprehensive training in reconciliation including provision of a spreadsheet that incorporates the concepts discussed in this chapter. If you are interested in learning more about Owner Proactive Strategies, reach out to us and we will be happy to discuss how we can help you create an efficient oversight approach.

Other Month-End Activities

In addition to reconciling deposits against collections, there are a few other things that need your attention at month-end:

1. While it is a bit more labor intensive, it is a really good idea to verify that the subcomponents of your deposits (i.e., cash, checks, credit card payments etc.) line up with the totals from practice management software.

2. Review the statement from your credit card merchant services provider. Every refund or credit processed through your merchant account should have a corresponding entry in your practice management software. The slight challenge is that the merchant services statement does not provide the identity of the patient or responsible party. However, the date

the refund was processed according to the merchant statement should give you a pretty good clue as to the date in practice management software.

3. The month-end is also the time to look at some specific reports from your practice management software. I will repeat my earlier advice; any reports you rely on should be those you have printed yourself. The following are some reports worth reviewing each month. Depending on the practice management software you are using, they may have slightly different names in your software, but you will get the idea:

   a. Production report.
   b. Deleted transactions report.
   c. Modified transactions report.
   d. Adjustments report.
   e. Receivables report. You should print three versions of this report; the standard version and another with credit balances excluded, and a third that provides receivables by provider.

Why should you look at receivables in two ways, with credit balances filtered for one of them? Doing so prevents someone from masking overdue balances by creating "phantom" credit balances. Let's say that a patient has a balance of $900 that has been paid by the patient or insurance company but then was stolen. It is often less conspicuous for a thief to create a phantom credit for $900 (which offsets the $900 debit balance to make a net balance of zero) than to do a more visible transaction to write off the debit balance. The result of a phantom credit is that the patient's balance nets to zero and will not appear on the receivables report. Filtering out credit balances can give a much clearer picture of receivables than looking at a "net" report.

In some cases, phantom credit balances may also interfere with the correct "aging" of the receivables by the practice management software.

When looking at the receivables by provider, be on the lookout for situations where a patient or family has a credit balance with one provider and a debit balance with a different provider. Some embezzlement patterns can cause this phenomenon, and it can also be indicative of posting errors by your team. Particularly if you have providers who are paid on collections, errors like this can end up over or undercompensating providers.

Chapter 14 discussed how the fractured accounting system used in practices facilitates embezzlement and makes your accountant ineffective at finding embezzlement. A proper month-end oversight effectively forces convergence between your practice management software and the accounting process.

18

Unauthorized Adjustments and Robin Hood Fraud

We frequently see staff at dental practices adjusting patient accounts that fall outside of the established policies for discounts.

Broadly these discounts fall into three categories:

1. Discounts entered into practice management software that are used to cover amounts stolen by the staff member. This is simply a concealment for embezzlement.
2. Discounts accorded to the family and friends of the thief, possibly with a *quid pro quo* back to the staff member.
3. Discounts granted to people who are not identifiable as family or friends. Earlier, we labeled this phenomenon as "Robin Hood" fraud.

The first two actions are just forms of embezzlement. Robin Hood fraud is not, although it is still theft and is prosecutable.

The question that merits some discussion with a criminal act that does not provide a direct benefit to the person committing the act is why they do it. I've often said that I understand why people steal but I'm puzzled at why people make graffiti. In contrast to stealing, which economically benefits the thief, graffiti actually costs the perpetrator money. You need to buy a can of spray paint, plus seemingly an entire "gangsta" wardrobe (including $300 sneakers) before putting your "tag" on a bus stop. People make graffiti either to destructively express their anger at a system, or to stroke their ego when they put their marked for everyone to see and admire.

I think that Robin Hood fraud is the dental office equivalent of graffiti. It carries some level of risk, for no economic reward.

So why do people commit this act? There are a few possible reasons:

- Possibly there is a relationship between the parties that has not been identified. For example, Prosperident was once involved in a case where a staff member wrote off a patient's balance in exchange for a new set of car tires. If this is the case, it was not actually Robin Hood fraud.
- The staff member is attempting to make the practice look better statistically. By removing some accounts receivable from the books certain key performance indicators can look better. If a bonus plan is in effect

for this staff member, these actions might be motivated by an attempt to manipulate the bonus program.
- The staff member dislikes asking patients for money and their fraudulent actions allow this to be avoided.
- Granting discounts may allow the staff member to elevate themselves in the eyes of the patient, while simultaneously diminishing the patient's view of the ("greedy") doctor.
- This is an act of revenge against someone that the staff member views as overpaid and avaricious.

Making unauthorized adjustments, even when the staff member does not receive a discernable benefit, is normally still a crime. What the crime is called varies a bit across jurisdictions, but it is normally categorized as either larceny or the broad category of theft.

Larceny had its origins in common law, where law was defined by court cases rather than statutes. The common-law concept of larceny addressed theft of tangible property only and did not cover the theft of intangibles. This probably made sense, because the economic role of intangibles was probably far less in the Middle Ages than it is today.

As legal systems matured, much of what was originally common law got "codified" into statutes. In doing so, most jurisdictions have broadened the definition of larceny to include theft of services and other intangibles.

19

Handling Bad Debts

One of the unfortunate facts of like about being a dental practice owner is that not everyone pays the amount they owe to the practice. In addition to financial losses, staff time, and some bruxism on your part, bad debts often form a convenient place for a thief to hide what they have stolen.

Here are some considerations when handling your bad debts:

1. Conceptually, let's differentiate "write-offs" from other types of adjustments. When you make most adjustments, for example, a Preferred Provider Organization adjustment, you are doing so because the amount being adjusted was never collectible. In contrast, a bad debt write-off is done because an amount you originally thought was collectible turned out not to be.

2. For this reason, the process of doing bad-debt write-offs is never a time-sensitive one and should be scheduled to be done periodically. Quarterly is plenty, and staff should never be running to you needing an "urgent" write-off to be approved.

3. Assuming that you are using the cash method for accounting (see the discussion in Chapter 14), there is no tax implication from doing a write-off. Under the cash method, you are taxed when you receive money, which clearly hasn't happened for accounts you are about to write off.

4. Contrary to what many dentists believe, the process of writing off a balance does not extinguish the debt. The patient still owes you the money, and your ability to take recovery steps is not diminished in any way by the process of removing the debt from your accounting system.

5. Every debt being written off should have lots of collection activity evident in the chart visible to you before you approve it. This person should have been called several times, a letter or two sent, and probably a text message as well before the practice recognizes the work you did on this patient as free dentistry.

6. If the dollar amount is significant (you can decide on the threshold, but probably $500 is a good number), you should try to call the patient yourself before you give up. Sometimes staff gives up too quickly before wanting something taken off their plate, and let's not

forget the magic that the word "doctor" sometimes produces.

7. Often write-offs are an indicator of a failure in your practice's systems. Sometimes a patient is caught in circumstances that make them incapable of paying. At other times, they received a much larger bill than anticipated, or they are unhappy with the dental work that was done, and not paying is their way of communicating their anger.

8. Watch what I call "soft" write-offs carefully – these are patients where insurance was supposed to pay and did not, and now the balance is being extinguished. This write-off may mean that your staff did not follow up with an outstanding insurance claim, and now the claim has become stale-dated.

9. For any patient for whom you are writing off money, check that their chart, and those of any family members, are flagged in your practice management software to prevent them from being reappointed. When patients do get reappointed after stiffing you, this represents a huge red flag for embezzlement.

10. The question arises of how to account for patients who are sent to a collection agency. Some practices perform a full write-off when accounts are sent to collection. Others leave the accounts on the books until the amount, if any, to be recovered by the collection agency is known and then write off the remaining balance. I don't love either of these approaches; the first causes these patients to be forgotten. The second approach

results in amounts that will never be collectible staying on your books, even if the collection agency makes 100% recovery.

When sending a balance to collection, my suggestion is that process a write off for the collection's agency's percentage. If a collection agency charges you 30%, as soon as you send an account to that agency, you have relinquished that 30% of the balance owing. You can recognize this loss now and, depending on the collection agency's success, deal with any further write-off later.

Unfortunately, bad debts are an area that many dentists leave totally in the hands of staff, which is generally unwise.

20

Some Other Protective Steps

Enter Treatment in the Operatory

Before practices computerized, treatment performed by a dentist or hygienist was recorded on a paper chart. When a patient finished treatment, their chart was carried to the front desk for a receptionist to transcribe what was performed into the manual "pegboard" system used to track production and receivables.

When practices computerized initially in the 1990s, early practice management software did not replace paper charts (and computers had not yet made it into operatories) so the practice of treatment being entered by front-desk staff continued.

However, decades later there are still practices using a "routing slip" or old-fashioned paper charts to communicate what treatment was performed to the front desk staff, who enter this treatment into practice management software. There are several issues with this practice:

1. It is inefficient. There is a duplicated effort when someone needs to transcribe what someone else entered.
2. It is error prone. While many front-desk staff have clinical experience, many others do not. The requirement to read someone else's handwriting creates potential for errors. Furthermore, clinicians expecting front desk staff often use descriptions instead of CDT codes to document their work, and there are often subtle differences between procedures that a front-desk team member, especially without a clinical background may not identify.
3. Clinicians entering treatment into practice management software make embezzlement more challenging. We discussed in Chapter 12 the desire for thieves to keep patient account balances accurate when stealing. When a patient finishes treatment and checks out at the front desk, if treatment has already been entered by clinicians, this patient already has a balance owing to the practice for that treatment in practice management software. If amounts paid by that patient are going to be stolen, now the thief must deal somehow with that existing balance. Whatever transaction is used to eradicate this balance is visible (is how we catch many thieves in investigations).

4. On the other hand, if a patient standing at reception has a zero balance (because treatment has not yet been entered), a would-be thief has several additional options for stealing and keeping the patient's account balance accurate, and the embezzlement is far more difficult to spot.

Having treatment entered by clinicians in operatories is an important part of the "division of duties" between staff that will be discussed in more detail in Chapter 20.

Handling of Cash

One mistake that many practices make is to co-mingle "float cash" with "petty cash." Float cash is what is used to make change when patients pay with cash. There should be a stipulated amount of float cash (for example, $500), and the daily starting and ending float balance should be identical. If the stipulated amount is $500, and at the end of the day, there is $1,320 in the drawer, $820 in cash was received that day. The $820 is segregated for a deposit (and it needs to balance to the practice management software's total for the day for cash payments), restoring the float to the $500 with which it should start tomorrow and every day. Under no circumstance should cash in this drawer be used for any purpose other than to make change for patients.

A second cash supply, called petty cash, normally sits in a locked drawer in the office manager's office. The purpose of petty cash is for when the office is required to pay some outlay in cash (or bail the doctor out when he or she forgot their wallet at home and needs lunch money). This cash also has a specified amount (for example, $200), and the office manager is responsible for keeping cash and receipts that always total $200. When the hungry doctor gets $20 for lunch, a $20 IOU is placed in the petty cash drawer. When the office runs low on stamps, and someone goes to the post office to buy some, that person provides the receipt in exchange for reimbursement from petty cash. When the amount in petty cash gets low, the office manager totals up the receipts on hand and "sells" them back to the practice. The doctor signs a check in an amount equal to the receipts, which, once cashed by the office manager, will bring the total petty cash back to the $200 stipulated amount.

When practices fail to maintain separate petty cash, it is very easy to lose control of the cash drawer, with the consequence that it becomes a nightmare to balance. Maintaining separate float and petty cash makes this process a snap.

Dentists Who Pocket Cash

Giving in to the temptation to put cash received from patients into your pocket while bypassing the books (and the IRS) can make it much harder to have an embezzler prosecuted. We discuss the issues with putting yourself in a position where you can be blackmailed in Chapter 5, but there is a second issue with helping yourself to cash. Unless the practice owner keeps a detailed record of the cash that he or she took in this way, if an embezzler is stealing cash, it will quickly become difficult to separate what was taken by the embezzler from what was taken by the practice owner. Resist the temptation.

Will a Check Scanner Help Protect Me?

I get asked this question a lot. The answer is no. A check scanner is simply an alternative way for a check to arrive at your bank, no more and no less. If I plan to steal one of your checks, I will simply make sure that check is not scanned.

This question is instructive in a couple of ways. First, it reflects the mistaken belief that the danger to a bank deposit is what might happen between when it leaves the practice and when it arrives at the bank. As discussed in Chapter 17, the true danger occurs when the practice owner fails to compare collections according to practice management software with what was deposited. Not monitoring collections versus deposits will allow the dumbest and laziest thief imaginable to steal from you.

Second, the question reveals a blind faith in technological advances. We tend to assume that technology will somehow protect us from embezzlement. In fact, the reverse is true. Every technological innovation creates new opportunities for thieves. Eventually, the people who make the technology may plug some of the loopholes being exploited, but embezzlers normally manage to stay a step or two ahead.

You may be familiar with the movie (or the book that the movie is based on) called *Catch Me If You Can*. This autobiography is the fascinating story of Frank Abagnale, a forger and passer of bad checks in the 1960s. Frank's story is remarkable in several ways. He was a brilliant and successful criminal, and he evaded law enforcement for many years. And after being caught, he turned his life to the good and became a security consultant for the government and private industry.

His amazing ability to understand the habits and thought processes of his victims makes his book required reading for newly hired Prosperident investigators.

Frank's perspective on technology is instructive. In a 2019 interview, he said the following:

> "What I did 50 years ago as a teenage boy is 4000 times easier to do today because of technology. Technology breeds crime. It always has, and always will."[53]

Destroy the Signature Stamp

There was a time years ago when signature stamps performed an important function in practices. With many insurance claims being submitted in paper form, the stamps eliminated the dentist's need to perform the tedious task of manually signing every insurance claim.

With almost all claims now sent electronically and therefore not requiring signatures, the signature stamp is no longer

---

[53] Frank Abagnale interview with techrepublic's Karen Roy, August 12, 2019 https://www.techrepublic.com/article/famous-con-man-frank-abagnale-crime-is-4000-times-easier-today/

needed for what was once its primary function. Since signature stamps can create lots of mischief in a larcenous employee's hands, you should destroy all signature stamps in your office.

Learn Your Practice Management Software

A subset of dentists appears to believe that they will catch a communicable disease if they get too close to the practice management software that silently lurks in a dark corner of their office. I can tell you categorically that there are no fatalities associated with practice management software. If you have this "technophobia", it's time to get over it. As I suggested earlier, the software is not going away, and it's time for you to acknowledge its permanence and learn some of the basic functions in your software. There are lots of places to acquire this knowledge. No excuses – get it done.

Control Over Incoming Mail

A basic precaution that you can take is to gain control over the incoming mail. This step makes certain embezzlement types much harder and may create a bit of mystery about what your supervisory process really is. I recall a million-dollar embezzlement case that we investigated. The doctor had set up a special-purpose account that was used for a certain type of revenue. About a year after this was done, the office manager realized that her doctor had totally forgotten about this account and began plundering it. How did she know this? The office manager was the person who received and sorted the mail.

Every month like clockwork, the bank sent a statement for this account, which the office manager dutifully filed away in her desk. Eventually, she realized that the doctor had never asked her for those statements, which is when she began treating this account as her own piggy bank.

And by control of the mail, I mean **exclusive** control. Several practice owners have told me that they control the mail, but when I probe a bit deeper, it turns out someone else receives the mail and then puts it on the doctor's desk. It doesn't occur to the doctor that the embezzler has picked over the mail before the doctor sees it. I expect that more than a few flyers giving notice of an upcoming event where I am speaking about embezzlement have gone in the garbage before an embezzler puts the rest of the mail on the dentist's desk.

To handle mail properly, it needs to go either to a post office box that only you have the key for or to your home. This practice ensures that you are truly the first person to see the mail. Also, you need to open everything except obvious junk mail; passing a piece of mail unopened to a staff member makes it clear that you didn't look at it.

Banks and an increasing number of other entities have "gone green" and are now sending statements electronically instead of by mail. Handling these statements requires similar thinking. Statements should go to your personal email address and not an administrative office address. When you forward a statement to someone else for action, don't forward the entire email, including the attachment; this is the equivalent of handing someone an unopened envelope. Please take a couple of seconds to copy and forward the attachment without the covering email that brought it to you. This method communicates to the recipient that you have looked at the attachment.

Assignment vs. Non-assignment Practices

I am frequently asked whether practices that accept insurance benefits are more prone to embezzlement than non-assignment practices.

While most readers will know this, for each insurance claim submitted to an insurance company, the practice has the option of directing the insurance payment to the practice or the patient. Most practices normally direct insurance payments to the practice and collect only the co-payment portion from patients with insurance, which is known as assignment.

The direct billing of insurance in this fashion presents numerous administrative issues for practices. For example, it is often a challenge to accurately determine the amount of the co-payment until after the insurance check is received, so this means that any amount collected at the time of treatment is necessarily an estimate, with final determination able to be made only after the insurance money has been received.

Collecting an estimated copayment at the time of treatment often has the effect of leaving the patient with a small debit or credit balance, which must then be addressed. Alternatively, offices may choose to wait until insurance funds have been received before collecting from the patient so that the exact amount owing by the patient is known. However, this increases the practice's receivables and creates the administrative effort needed to produce and mail statements. Furthermore, it is far more likely to collect money when a patient is standing at the front desk after treatment than to invoice them later.

Some insurance companies will only allow an insurance claim to be assigned to a dental office if the dentist is "in network" with them. Failing to collect the full amount from a patient where assignment is not possible creates the potential for the patient to receive an insurance payment and use the money for some other purpose than paying the dentist.

Accepting insurance payments assignments also tends to position dental offices as unwilling intermediaries between patients and their insurance companies. When an insurance company doesn't pay, the task of following up (and the pain of carrying the unpaid balance) belongs to the office, whereas in a practice that does not accept assignment, non-payment from insurance is the patient's problem. Also, in an assignment office, if insurance doesn't pay or pays some amount other than expected, the office tends to get blamed and is often under some pressure from the patient to write off any balance that results from the insurance company not doing what was expected.

For these reasons, most dentists consider becoming a non-assignment practice to be desirable. However, market pressures often make refusing assignments a utopia that they probably will never achieve. In my experience, the only practices that can succeed as non-assignment practices are in one of two categories; either they are a monopoly (for example, the only oral surgery practice in a 50-mile radius), or they focus on high-end cosmetic procedures that aren't covered by insurance.

As far as its relationship with embezzlement goes, I don't think accepting or not accepting assignments provides the practice owner with any advantage. In other words, the likelihood of embezzlement is equal for a non-assignment practice compared to an assignment practice. As I have suggested in Chapter 5, embezzlement is far more driven by the pressures facing the embezzler than any practice-specific factors.

The methodology used to steal differs between the two types of practices, at least when major theft occurs. In an assignment practice, insurance checks are easy to steal, and no insurance company pays any attention to who cashes their checks. Non-assignment practices typically take in more cash and credit card payments, and theft patterns in a non-assignment practice congregate around stealing cash and credit card payments made by patients.

The decision about whether to accept assignment should be based on factors other than the belief that a belief that embezzlement risk will be reduced.

Stored-Value ("Virtual") Credit Cards

Some insurance companies make payments to practices by creating virtual credit cards with credit balances and then providing the card numbers to practices. A practice can then enter the credit card number into its merchant terminal and receive payment.

Many dentists have reported that this arrangement was put in place without their consent and that opting out was not presented to them as an option.[54] Insurance companies favor this arrangement because it is more efficient for them than issuing checks or arranging ACH payments.

There are several disadvantages to allowing an insurance company to pay you in this way. First, when you process the payment through your merchant terminal, it is treated like any other credit card payment, and a processing fee of a couple of percentage points gets applied. This cost can be particularly galling in a PPO arrangement where you are already receiving contractually reduced fees.

While most dentists will swallow merchant account fees to provide added convenience to patients making payments, I'm not sure that paying these fees for a huge insurance company's convenience has the same appeal.

Second, many front desk staff struggle with how to enter this type of payment correctly into practice management software. Is it a credit card payment or an insurance payment? Unless a practice has a clear policy (and perhaps a separate payment code for these payments), it is entirely possible that different staff members in the same practice will take different approaches to recording these payments, causing a distortion in financial reporting and creating difficulties in balancing.

And finally, there are many possibilities for a larcenous staff member to abuse this payment system. Use of these cards is not

---

[54]   See a discussion of one dentist's experience at Dentists can opt out of credit card reimbursement from third-party payers, ADA News, October 2018, https://www.ada.org/en/publications/ada-news/2018-archive/october/dentists-can-opt-out-of-credit-card-reimbursement-from-third-party-payers

limited to a specific merchant terminal, so it doesn't take much imagination to conjure up abuse.

Even though individual insurance companies may not present this as an option, most states have passed laws preventing insurance companies from forcing you to accept payment via stored-value credit cards. If you are currently receiving payment in this manner, contact the insurance companies involved and opt out.

Smile for the Camera

I get asked this question a lot when I am speaking to groups of dentists: are cameras legal in my practice, and will they protect me against embezzlement? I have seen some consultants advocate cameras to counter embezzlement; their arguments center around deterrence and an increased possibility of detecting a thief.

Workplace cameras are normally legal except in "private" areas like restrooms, changing rooms, and, in some states, break rooms, if the purpose for recording is a legitimate one. However, most states require notification that recording is being done, so cameras hidden from employees (and patients) are generally not permitted.

Even if your jurisdiction permits hidden cameras, I think that installing them is a monumentally bad idea. Notwithstanding what you might see in the movies, permanently installed cameras require a certain amount of hardware. In addition to the lens and circuit board, they need a permanent power supply and a means of uploading their video to a computer where it can be stored and accessed. There is a decent chance that, sooner or later, a staff member will discover one of your artistically hidden cameras, and you can imagine the trust issues that will ensue when this happens.

The laws involving the recording of audio are considerably more stringent than those for capturing video. While it is usually legal to record surveillance video for legitimate purposes, audio recording is normally dealt with under "wiretapping" or "eavesdropping" laws. All states require the consent of at least one party to the conversation being recorded, with 11 states requiring the consent of all parties to a conversation. So even in situations where capturing video is legal, surreptitiously recording the audio probably is not.

A further consideration, if someone external to the practice has access to the video footage (e.g., your alarm monitoring company), the recorded video will almost certainly contain Protected Health Information, which means that you will need to obtain a Business Associate Agreement with the security company and whoever else would have access to the video to be compliant with privacy laws.

While front-desk cameras have their uses, such as deterring snatch and grab thieves who will enter businesses in the hope of finding the front desk unattended, the ability of cameras to catch embezzlement is minimal.

I will mention is that, although my team and I deal with hundreds of embezzlement cases each year, the number of times we see a thief caught on camera in one of our investigations in a year is normally zero, despite working in numerous offices where cameras are present.

Here are a few of the reasons why cameras are ineffective at stopping embezzlement.

1. Unless you see someone taking payment from a patient and stuffing it into their pocket or purse, everything else captured on camera is difficult to categorize as embezzlement. Since you are normally required to make staff and patients aware that you are recording, it would be an uncommonly stupid staff member that does this in view of the cameras.

2. Thieves adapt. Suppose you have undetected embezzlement taking place, and you install cameras and provide the notice that your state probably requires you to. In that case, a thief will develop a plan to continue embezzling that avoids being caught on camera. Judging from our observations, they are very likely to succeed.

3. Ongoing monitoring is virtually impossible, and any thief realizes this. Cameras are useful for events when the time of the event can be approximated. If, for example, a computer monitor is stolen from your reception area, it is normally possible to determine within a short time window when that event took place, so it is easy to review video footage and see the theft on video.

    However, embezzlement can happen at any time, so the amount of video you would have to watch to keep an eye on your staff is enormous. If your office is open for 35 hours per week and you need two cameras to cover front desk activity adequately, you are capturing

70 hours of video per week. When are you planning to watch it? Even sped up by a factor of 5, you would need to devote 14 hours per week to watch the video to look for that elusive few seconds of embezzlement activity, which is a commitment that most dentists will not make.

4. Recording video without capturing the audio often makes it difficult to determine the context of whatever your front desk person is doing. It is unlikely that you would ever be able to flag a specific action as embezzlement from video only. The security video's resolution is normally insufficient to see, for example, the details on a computer monitor or the specific keystrokes entered by a staff member.

5. Video consumes a lot of computer storage, so most systems retain a limited amount of past video and then overwrite it with more current footage. Typically, the amount of video retained is less than a month, which means that even if you wanted to look at video from six months ago, it is probably no longer available.

Division of Duties

Embezzlement normally has two components. There is the "conversion" where the doctor's property ends up in the possession of the thief. Then there is "concealment" where the fact that money is missing is artfully hidden from the practice owner.

One of the best tools for frustrating the concealment of theft is a proper division of duties in a practice.

We see many embezzlement situations where the trusted office manager "handles everything" and doing so enables them to both steal and then conceal the losses.

There are five basic tasks in the flow of money through your practice:

1. Recording treatment (which should be done by clinical personnel in operatories – see the discussion in Chapter 20),
2. Receiving payments, either by mail or "over the counter."
3. Recording the payments in practice management software.
4. Depositing the funds to the bank.
5. Balancing (i.e., the action taken at the end of the day to ensure that collections according to practice management software correspond with the amount deposited to the bank as Discussed in Chapter 17).

I'm going to give you two simple rules for dividing duties among your team:

1. No staff member should perform more than two of these five functions. If you have a big office with plenty of staff, this is easy to accomplish. If your staff consists of you, an assistant and a receptionist, it is considerably more challenging and will result in you or your spouse personally taking on some of these tasks.

2. The two tasks that an individual staff member performs cannot be consecutive. So, the person who gets and opens the mail should not be the person who posts the insurance checks to practice management software. The person who does day-end balancing should not be the person who makes bank deposits. And so on.

Look at what each person in the "money chain" does in your practice and redistribute as needed to follow these rules. As mentioned, in a small practice, it is virtually inevitable that the doctor personally performs some of these tasks to achieve a proper division.

Also, let's acknowledge a basic limitation of even a proper division of duties. There is a big unspoken assumption underlying rationale to divide responsibilities. This assumption is that most would-be embezzlers are reluctant to approach a co-worker to invite that colleague to participate in an embezzlement scheme. Most of the time, this assumption is correct. Typically, the co-worker's reaction is unknown, and an embezzler asking a colleague for help to steal runs a significant risk of being turned in to his or her boss. However, the place where this assumption breaks down is when the would-be embezzler and their co-worker have a relationship that extends beyond the workplace. For example, they may be related to each other or be close friends outside the office. A strong relationship increases the predictability of a response and lessens the risk posed by inviting another staff member to participate in dishonesty.

In these circumstances, collusion is a possibility. One chilling statistic from the Association of Certified Fraud Examiners is that the median amount stolen doubles when a conspiracy is involved.[55]

While I would never discourage a dentist from hiring friends or relatives of existing staff, one consideration when dividing duties is whether collusive fraud might be a possibility. Also, one caution I would raise is when you are looking at hiring someone, and you discover (through social networking, perhaps) a heretofore undisclosed friendship between the applicant and an existing employee.

If someone is applying for work at your practice and knows someone who is already working there, the applicant should usually be keen to tell you that, with the belief that this friendship might increase their chances of being hired. It is also the practice of many dentists to canvas existing team members to ask if they know anyone who would be a suitable hire for the practice, in case they know someone who would be a good fit.

When the first knowledge of such a friendship comes indirectly, you must consider the possibility that the existing employee and the applicant have a hidden agenda and that their plans could include collusive fraud. I'll address hiring more fully in Chapter 22.

If you have established effective daily and monthly monitoring systems, this will not prevent embezzlement. However, you have made it considerably more difficult and dramatically increased the probability of spotting it.

---

[55] "ACFE Report to the Nations: 2018 Global Fraud Study." *ACFE*, www. acfe.com/report-to-the-nations/2018/. Accessed 30 July 2019.

21

Improvise, Adapt and Overcome: Inside the Mind of the Embezzler

One of my favorite movies is Heartbreak Ridge from 1986, in which Clint Eastwood plays battle-hardened Marine Gunnery Sergeant Thomas Highway. He frequently incites his Marines, in his distinctive gravelly voice, to "improvise, adapt, and overcome" when faced with a problem. While an embezzler in your practice may not have served in uniform, they have probably adopted GySgt Highway's mantra wholeheartedly. As a group, they display considerable resourcefulness when solving the problem of how to steal from you.

For example, while stealing cash is the first choice of every embezzler, when an embezzler is constrained by the amount of cash taken in by a practice, they will smoothly evolve to stealing checks, credit card payments, or direct deposits to your bank account. While it is less common, theft of consumables, scrap gold, or even dental equipment also happens, but our focus in this discussion will be the theft of monetary items.

When a specific methodology of concealing their theft is blocked, they will improvise, adapt, and overcome to find a different way.

Chapter 3 discussed the two types of thieves, Needy and Greedy, and the three preconditions for theft, Pressure, Opportunity, and Rationalization.

If a would-be thief has the three necessary ingredients of pressure, opportunity, and rationalization, what happens next? The answer is that they begin to study their adversary, and that adversary is you! They can usually construct a highly accurate profile of what you scrutinize in your practice, and more importantly, what you do not, to build an embezzlement plan that bypasses your scrutiny.

It is an unequal battle. Your clinical responsibilities keep you busy, and running your practice is often something you sandwich between patients. On the other hand, your adversary, the embezzler, has all day to study you and get to know your habits.

It is kind of like playing poker with someone and your cards are face up and theirs are hidden. Even a much smarter player will probably lose money at that poker table.

What does work? You are far from powerless against this problem, but you need to take an approach that is somewhat different than what the self-appointed experts prescribe. Here are some very effective strategies:

1. Screen applicants carefully before you hire them. One of the best ways to protect yourself from embezzlement is to keep dishonest people from getting jobs in your practice. I will cover my suggestions for better hiring practices in Chapter 22.

2. Behave ethically. Suppose you cut corners in a way visible to staff, such as cheating on income taxes, cutting corners with your patients' insurance coverage, or having an extramarital affair with a staff member. In that case, you create a situation where someone can embezzle from you without fear of consequences because of the potential damage they can do to you.

3. Observe staff behavior. Studies show that over 90% of embezzlers display some behavioral markers of their improper activity.[56] Many embezzlers work extra hours, do not take a vacation, or are unusually possessive about their workspace or duties. While financial problems do not automatically lead to stealing, they can create the "pressure" to steal that I talked about in Chapter 4. Certainly, addictions of any kind are a cause for concern. Prosperident sells an inexpensive Embezzlement Risk Self-Assessment Questionnaire in our online store that facilitates the process of monitoring employee behavior, which you can access at https://www.prosperident.com/store/. I'll discuss behavior in more detail in Chapter 30.

---

[56] "2016 ACFE Report to the Nations." *2016 ACFE Report to the Nations*, www.acfe.com/rttn2016/perpetrators/red-flags.aspx.

4. While "denial of opportunity" strategies do not tend to have much success, what does work without consuming excessive amounts of your time, is **monitoring**. For example, rather than take the bank deposit to the bank yourself, a verification that the correct amount arrived at the bank is equally effective and requires far less time. The daily and monthly oversight steps that I covered in Chapter 17 are a good place to start.

5. One area where you need to be particularly careful is in marketing programs that involve discounts on services. What may happen is that patients who are unaware of the programs end up paying full price, with a staff member entering the fee into the practice management software at the discounted amount and pocketing the amount of the discount.

One of the real ironies about this topic is that, superficially, embezzlers present themselves as ideal employees. In part, this is because stealing can be time-consuming, so these employees tend to work extra hours (which often gets misinterpreted by the dentist as loyalty). Also, many embezzlers deliberately worm their way into your life, and your thief becomes the person who babysits your kids or runs your errands on his or her lunch hour. Embezzlers want you to believe that your office, and maybe even aspects of your personal life, could not possibly function without them. As soon as they get you thinking in that way, their ability to steal from you increases dramatically.

Many thieves work extra hours due to the time burden of stealing and may be reluctant to draw attention to the extra work time by claiming overtime pay for it, so be alert for staff apparently "donating" their evening and weekend time to the practice.

While some embezzlers will spend extra time in the office to perform their stealing, others are not interested in replacing the time that they divert to pilfering, and the consequence is that their official duties suffer. When an employee is deciding how to spend the next work hour, and their choices are to do something that makes money for the practice or to do something that enriches them, your interest may not always prevail.

One thing that will surprise many dentists is that particularly when someone is doing what was labeled in Chapter 11 as "concealment theft," keeping track of the adulterations they have made in your practice management software becomes challenging. Some thieves will make use of something investigators call a "cheat book," where they keep track of the false entries they have made. Back in 1989, when I started, typically, this was a notepad. I solved one of my earliest cases when I looked for and found the embezzler's cheat book. In the modern era, the cheat book more likely takes the form of an Excel or Word file on the embezzler's computer.

22

Please, Please Do Not Hire an Embezzler

Doctors Hate Hiring, and Thieves Know This

When I speak with live audiences of dentists, I often ask for a show of hands from those audience members who enjoy hiring staff. It probably will not surprise you that usually, no one in the audience raises their hands. Hiring staff is difficult and a task that many dentists thoroughly despise.

Economic conditions dictate whether you receive 100 applications or only a handful for an employment vacancy you are hoping to fill, and both situations present challenges. When you have 100 applications, wading through enough resumes to fill a suitcase, and hoping to find the gem that is almost certainly buried there, is laborious. When very few people are interested in a time of low unemployment, none of the applicants may be precisely what you want. The challenge may be finding the least unsatisfactory employee and hiring them quickly before they get another job offer.

If you are like most of your peers and hate this entire process, the tendency may be to take shortcuts, along the lines of how my son approached cleaning up his room in his teens. The result is that most dentists know far less about people that they are about to hire than they should, and this offers an easy pathway for people who have already embezzled elsewhere into your practice.

There are many factors to consider when hiring. Aside from professional competence, you have an image and vibe in your practice that you want a new employee to reflect. You want someone who will mesh with the existing personalities in the office, including yours. Reading resumes, selecting people to interview, and then conducting those interviews can all be exhausting. Some factors overlay the process, such as the complex and sometimes evolving employment and anti-discrimination laws that apply to every hiring situation. There are often time constraints on this process. Many employees leave practices without providing much notice, and this leaves you trying to fill a vacancy quickly, and worse, doing so while trying to fit hiring in around seeing patients.

With this time pressure making events a bit of a blur, many dentists who are faced with needing to fill a position forget to step back and ask a fundamental question: is everything the applicant is telling me true?

To be clear, others are better equipped than I am to help you evaluate how well an applicant will perform their duties and the extent to which they will fit harmoniously into your practice. My focus is to help you avoid the employee who you really do not want to hire. My team frequently encounters "serial embezzlers," some of whom are as prolific as rabbits in mating season, and I have had lots of opportunities to see how they manage to hide their "baggage" and get hired by unwitting dentists.

The hiring challenge is broader than just avoiding embezzlers. Many people who would love to get hired by you are careless, toxic, lazy, or refuse to follow your rules, and none of these people plan to declare their unsuitability to you during the hiring process. And if you hate hiring and are anxious to get off the hiring treadmill as quickly as you can, you are playing squarely into their hands.

My purpose here is to help you uncover what an applicant does not want you to know about them. I will show you how to investigate someone properly before you offer them a job in your practice, and I will highlight some of the tricks that an applicant can use to hide an unsavory past.

Trusting Your Instincts is Dangerous

Traditionally, dentists have trusted their instincts when hiring staff and have eschewed the background checking techniques that are the norm in most other businesses.

For example, notwithstanding that over 60% of employers require applicants to test for drugs before being offered employment, very few dentists require them. Given the amount of money that can flow through a practice and the practice's ability to dispense controlled substances, this makes no sense whatsoever.

People with unsavory pasts are well aware of the laxity of the hiring process in dental offices. Internet chatter suggests that many people with "baggage" actively seek jobs in dentistry for this reason,[57] and this failure to vet applicants properly has cost many dental practices dearly.

What is always on my mind, and probably not in yours when hiring, is the question: what if what they are telling me is untrue, or if they are hiding something from me? Statistically, there is a pretty good basis for my concern.

The World is a Dangerous Place

There are a couple of numbers that should frighten every practice owner. First, over 70 million Americans (which equates to one in four adults) have criminal records.[58] To be clear, not **every** criminal record is a bar to hiring. Like any unfavorable information, it needs to be put into context. A record for marijuana possession from 20 years ago, with no criminal activity since then, might not stop me from hiring someone, whereas someone who just got out of prison for theft has no place in my office. The decision

---

[57] See, for example, "Can a Felon Become a Dental Assistant?" *Jobs*, 2010, www.indeed.com/forum/job/dental-assistant/Can-felon-become-dental-assistant/t233524.

[58] Natividad Rodriguez, Michelle, and Maurice Emsellem. "65 MILLION 'NEED NOT APPLY,' The Case for Reforming Criminal Background Checks for Employment." *The National Employment Law Project*, Mar. 2011, www.nelp.org/wp-content/uploads/2015/03/65_Million_Need_Not_Apply.pdf.

about whether a specific set of circumstances has implications for your practices is totally in your hands. What is important is that you made that decision based on complete information. It amazes me that most dental offices fail to do criminal records checks for all applicants. Ironically, the vetting done on me when I coached my son's ice hockey team for a couple of hours a week over a 20-week season was far more intensive than most dental offices use to screen employees.

The large number of people with criminal records doesn't tell the whole story. Chapter 29 discussed the likelihood that these people will re-offend, and that probability is stratospheric.

Another alarming statistic relates to the prevalence of resume falsification. Surveys consistently report that approximately half of all resumes contain some amount of false or misleading information. A 2015 study revealed that 46% of resumes contained false information, and, shockingly, 92% of college students surveyed admitted to lying on a resume.[59,60]

While I find this hard to believe, there are websites to help people "cook" their resumes and companies that, for a fee, will provide glowing but totally fake references for someone applying to work with you.[61]

---

[59]   Lake, Rebecca. "Beware: 23 Resume Falsification Statistics." *CreditDonkey*, www.creditdonkey.com/resume-falsification-statistics. html.

[60]   White, Martha C. "Resume Mistakes: More Than Half of Hiring Managers See Lies on Resumes | Money." *Time*, Time, 13 Aug. 2015, www. time.com/money/3995981/how-many-people-lie-resumes.

[61]   See an example of a company that will provide glowing fake references here -- https://www.paladindeception.com/fake-job-references

How to Hire Properly

In this challenging environment, what is a dentist to do? Fortunately, there are some basic steps that you can take when hiring that will weed out most of the undesirables.

My first piece of advice is that some proactivity is needed when hiring. Every dentist understands the need for a "short notice list" to fill openings that arise in their schedule, and yet few extend the same concept to addressing staff vacancies. If you own a practice, sooner or later, you will need to hire, whether to replace someone who is leaving or to accommodate growth in your practice. Does it make any sense to wait until you urgently need someone to start looking? You encounter people all the time who would be a good fit in your practice. It is a great idea to begin noticing these people and, if appropriate, engaging them about the possibility of working with you in the future. Keep some notes about those you would like to go to when you need staff. Then when it happens, you are not starting "cold." Being proactive will make the hiring process more manageable and will yield better results.

Many dentists will confine their search to people with dental experience. Obviously, for clinical positions, this is a necessity. However, restricting yourself to filling administrative positions only in this way drastically narrows the pool of candidates and means that you may be overlooking those with the most potential.

Broadly there are two things that you want from a front-office person. On the one hand, you need them to know certain things about dentistry, dental insurance, and practice management software. The other requirement is for an outgoing personality, enhancing a patient's experience, and making them want to refer their friends. Ask yourself this question: which of these attributes is easier to teach and learn? Everybody who works in a dental office, including you, started with zero dental knowledge and managed to learn. However, turning an introvert into an extrovert is a monumental task. Suppose you are not naturally a trainer or do not personally have some of the knowledge needed to train someone for the position. In that case, there are plenty of training resources available, and the ability to access online training has made it much easier for dentists to train front office staff.[62]

Taming the Pile

If you are in the position of working through a large stack of resumes, there are a few strategies I use that may also help you. First, I apply some arbitrary rules to weed out the manifestly unqualified or undesirable.

1. I routinely discard a resume or cover letter with a single typo or grammar mistake. I assume that the written presentation in a resume and cover letter represents the absolute best that an applicant is capable of, and that errors present clear evidence of a literacy problem,

---

[62] My friend Laura Hatch has built an amazing business offering online front office training – check out her website at https://frontofficerocks.com/

and furthermore, a lack of awareness of the literacy problem.

2. I insist on resumes being transmitted to me by email. This requirement weeds out the few people who cannot use computers, a skill that is necessary for front office work in dental practices. If you are keeping the hiring process confidential, you can easily set up a single-purpose email address (e.g., dentaljobs4783@gmail.com) to use for this.

3. I use a more-or-less random posting number for any job posting, and I ask applicants to quote that posting number in their cover letters. Anyone who sends a cover letter without quoting the reference number lacks attention to detail.

4. I haven't gone to this level yet, but a friend of mine, Dr. Len Tau, uses an application process where applicants are taken to a website and must leave a 30-second video about themselves. This video provides another great opportunity to learn more about how an applicant presents themselves and their level of computer competence.

After applying these simple screening techniques, I look at the remaining resumes more closely to see who I believe can do the job and then get down to those I want to interview. And now the fun starts.

Once the clearly unsuitable have been weeded out using the strategies listed above, we need to extend our field of vision to accurately assess whether the skills an applicant lists on a resume are what we are seeking. Here are some measures to take to protect yourself against a hiring mistake.

Use an Application Package

You should have a job application package that all applicants are required to complete. Your HR advisors can help you develop a suitable template that gathers the necessary information while avoiding minefields like anti-discrimination legislation.

If necessary, in your state, your HR advisors can also assist with sequencing background checking properly. For example, some states as well as New York City have a "ban the box" law that prevents prospective employers from asking about a criminal record until after a conditional employment offer has been accepted. This requirement means that if you end up not hiring someone due to a criminal record, the basis for your decision was explicit because demonstrably, this person was suitable until the criminal record became known. This rule's rationale is to permit those with criminal records to have a fair shake at obtaining employment where the possession of a criminal record is not particularly job relevant.

Contrary to what some believe, criminal records checks in "ban the box" states are still permissible (and vital given that virtually every dental practice treats vulnerable segments of the population) so refusing to hire for your practice based on a relevant criminal record is not a problem in a "ban the box" jurisdiction. For hiring in dental offices, the effect of "ban the box" is really to set out a specific sequence that must be followed when investigating applicants, not to force a change in who you ultimately hire. The rule does, however, underscore the need for proper HR advice to avoid employment law pitfalls.

Second, your package can be used to obtain specific consents from the applicant for searches and investigative steps that you intend to perform. While in many states, the applicant's permission to contact former employers is implicit when they apply for employment with you, obtaining specific consent to do so is never a bad idea. More intrusive steps like credit checks and criminal record checks need to be conducted in accordance with state law and almost always must have the written consent of the job applicant.

The third benefit of using a job application form is that it facilitates comparison between applicants because everyone's information is presented in a consistent template.

Things to Check

Once you have decided who makes it to the interview stage, your first basic but important step should be to check their identification at the interview. All applicants must be able to provide you with a government-issued photo ID like a driver's license and at least one piece of other identification, such as a credit card or even a Costco membership or student ID. One of the easiest ways to hide an unsavory past when applying for a job, or to claim credentials that you don't really have, is to "borrow" someone else's identity. Someone who claims that they left their wallet at home is either lying or came totally unprepared for an interview and probably should not be hired.

Second, you **must** check work references from former employers. My rule is simple; I want to speak with every former employer the applicant has worked for in the past five years. No matter how well the applicant presents in an interview, do not, for any reason, skip this step. Many serial embezzlers are exceptionally good at encouraging their next "mark" not to bother checking references.

This vigilance isn't always easy. Sometimes for whatever reason, past employers are not available, and a bit of creativity is needed. A client of ours recently asked us this question:

> "I have an interviewee, and I would like to talk to her past employers. She's been at a national restaurant location for the last four years, but that location closed in April.
>
> "What would you recommend doing to check employment?
>
> "She listed three references from the restaurant with their contact info. Would you recommend contacting them?"

Our client is someone who makes every effort to run his practice properly, and his dilemma forces us to deal with a seminal issue in background checking – to whom should we be speaking?

Another challenge you may face is an applicant with work experience from an institutional employer such as a government department, hospital, or university. Often the information you can get from large institutions is limited by their internal policies.

The thought of having to make 3 or 4 phone calls to reach the person who can actually give you that limited information is sometimes discouraging. However, you must persevere. Often, people trying to hide negative work experience will falsely suggest that they worked for a large bureaucratic employer, hoping that you simply will not bother.

"Character References" are Useless

I often have dentists tell me that they ask for "references" or that they "check references." Normally they say this to show me that they are careful about who they hire. Typically, they ask the applicant for a list of people who the dentist can contact to gain some level of comfort about the applicant's character.

As I mentioned, the problem with many dentists' hiring practices is that they know far too little about the people they hire, so I am glad to see these dentists' willingness to close this knowledge gap. However, I think that by checking character references, their efforts are misdirected.

The first problem with applicant-supplied references is that they have been "cherry-picked" by the applicant. This bias means that the information they give you lacks objectivity. Everyone has at least a few people in their life who are raving fans, and when you call applicant-supplied references, that is exactly with whom you are speaking. Therefore, you are unlikely to hear anything remotely negative from these people.

I'm pretty sure that if my dog could talk, he would say wonderful things about me. Why? Because I feed him, go swimming with him and rub his belly on demand. However, he isn't exactly objective. What you want to avoid is speaking to the human equivalent of my pet.

To make the problem worse, often the references that are supplied (and checked) are in the nature of "character references," by which I mean that their knowledge of the applicant does not come from a work setting (e.g., their high school volleyball coach or parish priest). In addition to an objectivity issue, there are often other problems; the information you receive may suffer from a lack of relevance.

The people who can give you information that is both relevant and objective are former employers, and that is exactly with whom you should speak.

To circle back to my client's question, what is behind his query is what he (correctly) wants to do has been frustrated by the restaurant's closure.

In this case, because the applicant has nominated co-workers, the relevance issue is less important (because these people have observed the applicant at work and have done so recently). The true concern is objectivity.

Derivative References

My suggestion to the client was to call the supplied references to ask if they supervised or managed the applicant. If the answer to this question was no, then who were the applicant's supervisor and manager? I would then call these people to ask about the applicant. We refer to this concept as obtaining **derivative references**.

Particularly if the applicant's supervisor and manager were not on the supplied list of references, now, I would have access to information that is more likely to be objective. In cases where it is difficult to access former employers directly, keep the derivative references concept in your toolbox.

The danger is that there may be one or more jobs the applicant had where he or she knows that, if you spoke with that former employer, you would not want to hire the applicant, so the applicant will contrive various ways to encourage you to skip having a conversation with that employer.

Find their Phone Numbers Independently

Here is where you can outsmart dishonest people: do not call any phone number given to you by an applicant. If you do, you might end up speaking to a relative of the applicant pretending to be a former employer. Using your favorite online search engine and independently finding the former employer's office's telephone number is a much wiser option. Once you contact an applicant's former employer, make sure you speak with the decision-maker and not a co-worker of the applicant. If the previous employer is a dental office, speak with the practice owner.

Once you get this person on the phone, here are the questions you should ask them:

1. Verify the **exact** dates of employment. Do not make the mistake of prompting a former employer with dates and ask for confirmation. Ask them an open-ended question like: "what was this person's start date at your

practice, and what was their last day of employment?" This question forces the former employer to look up and provide the dates for which you are looking, instead of simply agreeing with dates that you supply (which most humans would do if given a chance). Getting exact dates is essential, for reasons I will explain below. Also, be wary of resumes that lack detail. For example, listing only the year when specific jobs started and ended is a convenient way for an applicant to cover lengthy periods out of the workforce.

2. Confirm the applicant's job title. Compare what their former employer tells you to the title they have supplied you with in their application. Many applicants will overstate their job title in a previous position. Catching someone in this dishonest act will give you a pretty good preview of how much integrity to expect from them as your employee.

3. Try to confirm any salary information provided by the applicant. Although many employers may not discuss salary information, it never hurts to ask. This question is another chance to catch an applicant in an act of deceit.

4. Ask whether the applicant left on their own or if they were terminated. Many former employers will refuse to answer this question, but this should not deter you from asking.

5. The one question you must ask every former employer is whether they would rehire this person if they had a suitable opening. This question subtly uncovers a problem employee without putting a former employer

on the spot. By asking for a statement of future intentions, instead of specific information, you allow a former employer to say something unfavorable about the employer that is not dangerous to that former employer.

Another problem is that many former employers are reluctant to give negative, or sometimes any, information on an ex-employee. Particularly if the employer is in a state that gives qualified privilege to job reference information (see the discussion on qualified privilege in Chapter 22), it is good for you to know this and remind an employer you are calling if they seem reluctant to provide you with information. At a minimum, I would press a former employer to confirm employment dates, job title, and whether the employee is eligible for re-hire. One line I have used successfully with taciturn former employers is that "I'm letting you know that this applicant may be denied a job here because of your unwillingness to answer some basic questions." This tactic often serves to create visions of the person you call being sued by their former employer and may convince them to be a bit freer with information.

Don't Accept Written Reference Letters

Never, ever accept a written job reference without making a verification phone call (to the number you have determined independently, remember?). It is common practice for employees to help themselves to office letterhead when working to forge a reference letter for themselves after they have left their position or been fired. For that matter, ubiquitous color printers, and the availability of things like corporate logos on the internet, make forging letterhead and reference letters incredibly easy.[63]

Hidden Jobs

Aside from providing phantom references, there are a few other tricks that an applicant can use to frustrate your ability to get accurate information from former employers. The first is to omit one or more jobs from their resume.

In some cases, the applicant states that they were out of the workforce for that time, "traveling through Europe" or something similar. Your policy should be to require documentation for any absence from the workforce of more than 30 days. Someone who was in Europe should be able to produce a passport with entry and exit stamps from a European country, hotel receipts, digital photos, and other objective proof of their travels.

In other cases, the employment dates for some jobs are "stretched" to make other employment disappear from their resume. You're asking former employers for the exact employment dates is the easiest way to uncover this trick.

A third approach used to prevent you from learning the truth is to ask you not to contact the applicant's current

---

[63]   We have some guidance on how to review a resume critically, and an example of a forged reference letter at https://www.prosperident.com/how-do-serial-embezzlers-get-hired/

employer because "she/he does not know that I am leaving." This statement may be true, or it may be that the applicant was fired from that job two weeks ago, which they are now trying to conceal from you by pretending that they are still working there and unwilling to disturb their current work relationship. Your response to this concern should be along the lines of:

> "I understand the sensitivity, but I want to let you know that we do not hire anyone without speaking with their most recent employer. However, I am happy to postpone obtaining this reference to the very end of our process, so we will only contact your current employer after you know that you are our chosen candidate."

This statement will deter scammers but poses no threat to people asking for this consideration for legitimate reasons.

Can Psychological Testing Uncover Dishonesty?

Wouldn't it be nice if there was a psychological test that could measure someone's honesty?

In fact, these tests do exist. They are tests known as "integrity tests," and there are several of them that purport to measure the honesty of a subject. These tests normally consist of a set of questions designed to gauge the integrity of the person taking the test. The questions can include lifestyle questions about drug and alcohol use or questions like "What would you do if a store clerk handed you too much money in change?" or "Do you ever lie to your spouse?"

There are, however, several issues with these psychological tests for integrity. First, there is a paucity of independent research on the predictive validity of these tests. Most of the published studies have been conducted by the companies offering these tests.

Second, much of the research involves people taking tests in other than a job application situation. For example, several validation studies were done using prison populations as subjects, where test results were compared with criminal behavior. Like most psychological tests, a key tenet of testing is that the person taking the test wants to be properly assessed and therefore answers the questions truthfully. For someone with "baggage" seeking employment, this is a fatally flawed assumption.

The situational difference is key — prisoners taking such a test have no incentive to lie, whereas someone taking an integrity test for work has a clear motivation to answer the questions in a way that presents them in the best possible light. As you can see from the example questions above, the intent of the questions is quite transparent and the "right" answers are obvious.

One of the commercially available integrity tests makes the following statement on its website:

> When taking the Hire Success® pre-employment integrity test, all job applicants must acknowledge that they understand that

their answers are being considered as part of their application for employment with your company and that you will be relying on truthful answers to make a hiring decision. Lying on an integrity test or job application may be grounds for termination or not being considered for employment.

This statement seems to be a direct admission that the test's accuracy is dependent on test-takers answering truthfully.

A Princeton University study on psychological tests for integrity concluded that "the research on integrity tests has not yet produced data that clearly supports or dismisses the assertion that these tests can predict dishonest behavior."[64]

Since a considerable proportion of workplace stealing is never detected, the comparison data has an obvious contamination.

A study called "The Use of Integrity Tests for Pre-employment Screening," performed by the Office of Technology Evaluation of the United States Congress found that integrity test accuracy was between 37% and 64%.[65]

For these reasons, many of the errors from these tests are "false positive" errors, where the tests result in the rejection of people who do not have integrity issues. Especially in the

---

[64]   The use of integrity tests for pre-employment screening. (1990). Congress of the United States, Office of Technology Assessment, page 8.
[65]   Ones, D. S., Viswesvaran, C., & Schmidt, F. L. (1992). Meta-Analysis of Integrity Tests: A Critical Examination of Validity Generalization and Moderator Variables. *Defense Personnel Security Research Center*, page 48.

current climate of a shortage of qualified people to work in dental practices, rejecting suitable people makes an already challenging hiring environment even tougher.

The lack of reliability of these tests and possible cultural and racial bias has prompted the state of Massachusetts to ban psychological testing for integrity as part of employment screening.[66]

Any test where validity is predicated on truthful answers where certain applicants have incentive to lie is impermissibly flawed. Add to this the potential false-positive rejection of qualified applicants, and unfortunately, this kind of psychological testing is unlikely to prove itself useful.

A Proper Background Workup

In addition to doing thorough, and somewhat skeptical, reference checks, an identification check, drug testing, and criminal records checks that I mentioned previously, there are a few other things that should be part of every hiring decision:

1. Credit report. Particularly crucial for employees who will be handling money. And I'll mention that poor credit history does not necessarily mean that the person should not be hired. It means that you need to understand why this person has a poor credit rating

---

[66] Schaffer, D. J., & Schmidt, R. A. (n.d.). Personality testing: Do your pre-employment tests violate the ... - FindLaw. Personality Testing in Employment. https://corporate.findlaw.com/human-resources/personality-testing-do-your-pre-employment-tests-violate-the.html

and make an informed decision about whether their circumstances pose a risk to your practice.

For example, I view the poor credit rating of a single parent trying to exist on a dental assistant's salary differently than someone with poor credit who lives in a big house next to the golf course and drives a Lexus. People who live an extravagant lifestyle on borrowed money terrify me because when more conventional financing sources dry up, embezzlement may be where these people turn next.

2. Credential verification. This verification is essential for dental assistants, hygienists, and associate dentists. Do not accept a written credential; if online verification is possible, use it. Otherwise, you need to call the state licensing body to confirm that the credential is valid.

3. Education. Let's not forget that many people claim college degrees that they do not actually have when applying for employment or have purchased an online degree from a "diploma mill." A 2004 study suggested that 25% of job applicants overstate educational credentials, and yet surprisingly, only 34% of employers verify educational credentials.[67]

4. A social networking scan. This scan is a great way to learn more about an applicant. You can see their communication style and look for any expression of

---

[67] "LinkedIn Resume Fraud: Do Employers Check Degrees?" Gededucated.com, 16 Mar. 2015, www.geteducated.com/life-experience-college-degree/305-linkedin-professionals-found-listing-life-experience-degrees-on-resumes.

anti-employer sentiment or strong political views that may be inappropriate in your workplace. It is also an excellent way to search out red flag behaviors such as evidence of high-risk lifestyles and to uncover "time thieves" who are active on social networking during work hours.

It is also your chance to look for undisclosed friendships with existing staff members that may be a precursor to the collusive fraud that is discussed in Chapter 20.

5. Don't forget the basic tactic of entering the applicant's name into your favorite search engine to see what comes up. It is often worth trying first name and last name only and doing a second search using first, middle, and last names. In some search engines, surrounding your search names with quotation marks (e.g., "Sally Smith" and "Sally Marie Smith") will narrow down the number of hits that you get.

6. Prosperident maintains a list of about 700 embezzlers in our Hall of Shame. It's far from complete but merits a search. The Hall of Shame is at https://www. prosperident.com/prosperidents-hall-of-shame/.

I will mention that these are not "screening" techniques intended to reduce your pool of applicants down to something more manageable. These tools, which can cost money, take time, and are intrusive, should be used only after identifying your one preferred candidate. Once you have done that, then perform your vetting to ensure that you are getting precisely who you think you are.

The following diagram reflects a proper background workup on someone you plan to hire. Please feel free to compare it to how you currently investigate a possible employee.

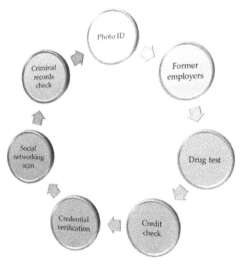

Figure 6 – A proper pre-hiring investigation

Once you have completed your screening, the next step is a written employment offer. As discussed, if you are in a "ban the box" state, this offer must take place before you check for criminal records. The offer should not be of the "cocktail napkin" variety. It should be designed by your HR advisors to conform to employment laws, not impair your ability to terminate at will, provide consent for ongoing due diligence (such as future drug testing while an employee), and of course, to state how the employee's compensation is to be determined.

My team frequently investigates payroll fraud cases, where an employee causes himself or herself to be overpaid. As I will discuss in Chapter 23, in the absence of a clear written agreement setting out how the employee's pay is determined, it can be challenging to obtain convictions.

"Chameleons"

The serial embezzlers described in Chapter 4 as fitting the narcissistic sociopath profile tend to perform well in the hiring process. They will send you a typo-free resume, which is rare in these days of pseudo-literacy, their sociopathy makes them outgoing and charming, and they will cater to that desire inside many dentists to be able to focus on their clinical responsibilities and leave the administration of the practice to someone else (we call this appealing to a dentist's "clinical fantasy"). When you hire these people, the reality is somewhat different.

I often describe serial embezzlers as chameleons. In the same way that the chameleon reptiles change their pigmentation to conform to their surroundings, serial embezzlers will research you and your office and go to some trouble to offer you what they have determined you are seeking. While you are interviewing them, they are also surreptitiously reverse interviewing you, which amounts to asking themselves how easy or hard it would be to steal from you.

To give you an example of how far they will go, one serial embezzler who has earned a place in our Hall of Shame was simultaneously applying for positions in general dental and orthodontic offices. When she applied for orthodontic positions, she would present a resume that suggested a decade of ortho practice experience. Concurrently, when she was trying to get hired by a general practice, she would offer a totally different resume that presented her work experience in general dental practices.[68] Also, as is common with serial embezzlers, this person would use different variations of her name when applying to keep her past from interfering with her job hunt.

Can Personality Testing Help Me Avoid These People?

Several personality profile tests are available to practice owners. Some of the better-known assessment tools are the DISC Assessment and the Briggs and Meyers Personality Test.

While profiling tools can be of considerable value in understanding your own personality better and hiring people who are more likely to mesh with your existing team, I think they are useless at identifying dishonest people.

All psychometric tests suffer from the same flaw in this regard; the assessment is done based on the subject's self-reporting. Therefore, the tests assume that the subject **wants** to be studied and that he or she is answering the questions honestly. Generally, in a profile-type assessment, it isn't hard to understand each question's purpose and, therefore, manipulate the outcome.

---

[68]   To see both resumes and our forensic discussion of them, have a look at our article at https://www.prosperident.com/how-do-serial-embezzlers-get-hired/

An organization approached Prosperident years ago, claiming that it had a test that could detect dishonesty, suggesting that this test might be used in what we do. I expressed my skepticism and was told that the test had been designed by eminently qualified clinical psychologists and was virtually foolproof. I recalled my father telling me when growing up that "foolproof" was elusive because fools can be quite ingenious, so I resolved to try to beat the test.

The company agreed to allow me to try their test, and I completed it twice. The first time, I answered every question that appeared to have an integrity element in a way that suggested that I was honest. The second time through, I answered the same questions differently. You can guess what happened; my honesty score on the first test was high, and it was abysmal on the second iteration. Since the same person (me) took the test both times, this variance of outcomes proves this kind of testing's fallibility.

Needless to say, after my demonstration, we never heard from this company again.

When It's Hard to Find People

One factor with which many dentists had to contend after the Covid pandemic was a chronic shortage of trained people available to work. The reasons for this "great retirement" have been discussed in the media, but regardless of why it happened, the lack of available and trained people posed some challenges for practice owners.

When you place an ad and only get a single response, it is tempting to forego pre-employment screening in the belief that a warm body is better than a vacancy. Don't think this way! Some adaptation may be necessary in times when good help is hard to find. You may be forced to lower your standards and hire people you would never bother with in times when more and better people are available. However, if you choose to relax your criteria for hiring, it is important to know by how much. If the applicant is an embezzler, or a child molester, the empty chair in your practice would have been far better, and pre-employment screening is what tells you the extent to which you are compromising.

One other reason practice owners provide for not checking into applicants in this climate is that they fear that if they dither and delay, some other employer with less screening will scoop the employee up. This fear may be justified when good people are hard to find, and there is a simple adaptation. Hire people probationarily and then perform your screening after they are hired. Ideally you would have this done before you ever bring someone into your practice but doing it (shortly) after hiring is far better than never doing the proper checks.

Hire Skeptically

I hope you get the idea that many people would like to work for you who should never get a job at your office. Bringing a skeptical approach to your hiring process and using the verifications applied in most other businesses dramatically reduces your chance of making a huge hiring mistake.

23

Compensation Fraud

Paying an employee involves the application of a formula. The basic calculation involves applying a number of units (hours, for an hourly employee, or the fraction of a year, for a salaried employee) times a rate per unit. From there, modifications are made for source deductions, overtime hours, vacation entitlements, etc.

The calculation has become increasingly complicated over time, and you must deal with some exacting state rules, so many practices outsource the preparation of payroll.

Accordingly, compensation fraud can take two forms; it can be the adulteration of timekeeping records so that an employee is paid for more units than he or she actually worked, or it can involve the incorrect application of the payroll formula (improper hourly rate, application of overtime pay rate when straight time should have been used, improper vacation accrual, incorrect calculation of bonus entitlement, and so on).

Timekeeping Fraud

Timekeeping fraud is relatively easy to control. Biometric readers have become very inexpensive and will stop the practice of employees clocking each other in and out. All time entries should be reviewed and signed off by the employee's supervisor. This requirement means that if your office manager is paid hourly, the practice owner needs to review their hours. Regardless of the pay period used, time entries should be reviewed weekly. Longer review periods make it more difficult to correlate time entries with work schedules.

An end-of-process review is also required. This review normally involves checking the signed-off timesheets against what the payroll company used to prepare the payroll.

Finally, the timekeeping system needs to be "locked down" so that amending time entries is limited to very few people. My suggestion is that, in an office of 15 or fewer people, only the practice owner should have the ability to amend a time entry. This policy has the impact of forcing someone who forgot to clock in or clock out to appear in front of you to ask for a change, which will encourage people to pay attention. In a larger office, limiting this to the practice owner can become impractical, and it may need to be delegated down a level.

Payroll Calculation Fraud

Ask any prosecutor what about least favorite type of economic crime to prosecute, and most will tell you that it is payroll fraud. By its nature, this kind of fraud is normally carried out by the person to whom the authority to prepare payroll in the entity has been delegated.

What makes prosecution difficult is that dental practices are notorious for following sloppy HR practices. One glaring weakness is an absence of written employment agreements kept up to date as the parameters, such as hourly rates, change.

This laxity doesn't stop there and often extends to failure to conduct performance reviews, inadequate screening before hiring (see Chapter 22), and in many other areas.

A lack of structure in this area can hurt a practice owner when you believe that an employee has stolen from you by overpaying himself or herself. In the absence of a written employment agreement clearly specifying the basis for pay (i.e., hourly or salary), quantum, overtime entitlement if any, bonus participation, benefits, and the other details that go into the determination of an employee's correct compensation, with one exception prosecutions involving payroll calculation are destined to fail.

We all know that the probative standard in criminal matters is "proof beyond a reasonable doubt," which probably equates to 90% certainty. It is very unlikely that a judge or jury will find that level of certainty based solely on a difference of opinion between two credible witnesses, so a lack of documentary proof establishing what someone should have been paid will doom most prosecutions.

In the absence of a formal agreement, courts will certainly consider other evidence of what the actual arrangement between the parties was supposed to be. This evidence could include an employee manual, emails, informal agreements, or even an exchange of text messages. The danger in relying on any of these things is that they typically capture pieces of what is obviously a more complete arrangement between the parties. They are not a good substitute for a properly written, comprehensive employment agreement.

Employment Agreements

I sometimes hear discussions among dentists about whether employment contracts are a good thing to have or not, or whether they should be implemented in a doctor's practice. These discussions reflect a misunderstanding of contract law. Every employee has a contract. Some contracts are written, some are verbal agreements (collectively, these two are referred to as "express" contracts), and some are implied contracts.

The basic elements for a contract's existence are an offer by one party, an acceptance of the offer by the other, and both sides providing some form of "consideration" (defined as doing something you otherwise would not do if there were not a contractual relationship).

You probably have no reason to think of it in this way, but many everyday activities involve an implied contract. When you buy a loaf of bread at the supermarket, there is an offer (the price on the shelf by the bread), an acceptance (you picking up the bread and taking it to the cash), and consideration by both parties when you surrender your cash and the store parts with the loaf of bread.

These three elements are also present in every employment (or associate) relationship; employees show up to work, which is a consideration because they would not do this gratuitously. They get paid by the employer, also a consideration. The work performed and the amount paid are pursuant to some meeting of the minds (offer and acceptance) between the parties. Accordingly, every employee already has a contract, and all three types of contracts have the same legal significance.

Where the differences between these types of contracts matter is when there is a disagreement between the parties over what was agreed. Verbal and implied agreements suffer from both legitimate differences in interpretation and selective memory. A written agreement provides the only enduring record of what was agreed.

Also, with something as complex as a relationship of employment, a written agreement provides the only legitimate possibility for dealing comprehensively with the many issues that must be addressed. Unwritten employment contracts were probably perfectly sufficient at the time of the American Revolution. However, the employment relationship has become considerably more complex today, and leaving this complicated relationship to an unwritten agreement poses a sizeable danger.

The question for you as a business owner is whether you want to try to hold an employee to the terms of an implied contract, or worse, prove in court that the employee overpaid themselves compared to what was agreed.

I'll also mention that the legal system has an unspoken bias. When you delegate the authority to manage payroll to a staff member and then fail to supervise that staff member, you accept some responsibility for the consequences of that authority being abused. The courts tend not to reward business owners who fail to exercise prudence in running their affairs. The expression I saw one judge use in describing this situation is that the victim was the "author of his own misfortune."

I did mention one exception where prosecution is possible, even in the absence of a means to determine the correct entitlement to pay. I'm referring to situations where payroll theft involves an act of deception. Actively concealing the theft from the practice owner undercuts any argument that the thief was entitled to be paid what they took. For example, showing one payroll summary to the practice owner and sending a different one to the payroll company, for example, creates a situation from which the thief will have a difficult time wiggling out.

I frequently emphasize to our team that a successful conviction for payroll fraud requires "documentation or deception." Because many thieves who are padding their payroll are also stealing in other ways, sometimes the difficulty of securing a payroll-based conviction isn't necessary because we can identify plenty of other theft that is more readily prosecutable. However, when we take something to a District Attorney that involves nothing but payroll theft, we never expect a warm reception from the legal system.

Associate Agreements

I recently received a call from a practice owner who was asking for my advice. He was quite upset because an associate had left his practice and had opened one more or less across the street. My caller believed that his former associate was soliciting patients, and he was looking for me to validate his belief that this conduct was fraudulent.

I asked my caller what I thought was a very basic question about what the associate agreement said about solicitation of patients, and I was told that there was no written agreement. I was surprised. My question to my caller was this, "if you didn't want your associate to leave and take your patients, why didn't you put this provision in an agreement?" My caller did not have a good answer.

I'll make this simple. Associateship is a complex relationship, and there are many things that an associate can do that will harm your practice. This relationship is not one that should be concluded on a handshake or a "cocktail napkin" agreement. Get a proper written agreement.

24

How to Fire a Staff Member Properly

Most of us have seen or heard of a TV show called The Apprentice, in which its semi-famous host would scream "you're fired" on a weekly basis at an unfortunate contestant. The host eventually moved to a large white house at 1600 Pennsylvania Avenue in Washington, where he set a record for firing the most cabinet members in a president's first term of office.[69]

If only firing were that uncomplicated in a dental practice.

Employment at Will has Exceptions

Many dentists probably take more comfort than they should from the "Employment at Will" doctrine that is in place in 49 of

---

[69]   Lu, Denise, and Karen Yourish. "The Turnover at the Top of the Trump Administration." *The New York Times*, 17 Mar. 2018, www.nytimes.com/interactive/2018/03/16/us/politics/all-the-major-firings-and-resignations-in-trump-administration.html.

50 states (Montana is the exception; also, Canadian rules are very different). In its pure form, employment at will means that you can fire an employee at any time, for any reason, or even for no reason.

The problem with Employment at Will is that all states have carved out significant exceptions that make the principle far from absolute. Here are some of the important exceptions:

- Many employment agreements result in the parties agreeing to opt out of Employment at Will. Contractually requiring a certain amount of notice from an employee, for example, will mean that Employment at Will no longer applies.
- Many states have a public policy exception that protects employees from being let go who are making a Workers' Compensation claim or have entitlement under the Family and Medical Leave Act.
- Even in the absence of a formal written employment agreement, an implied contract may end Employment at Will. Casual statements from employer to employee such as "you have a job for life here" or "I'd like us to retire together" have been found to create such an implied contract.
- Many states impose a good faith requirement. For example, you are normally required to follow the terms of your employee handbook, and firing with the intent of disentitling someone to a bonus they would otherwise receive is not likely to be treated as an Employment at Will situation.

- A combination of state and federal laws prevents retaliatory terminations. So, an employee who just made a complaint to your state licensing body or OHSA is protected from termination.
- There is another big exception when a termination is determined to be discriminatory. Equal opportunities employment legislation establishes the following bases on which discrimination can be claimed -- race, color, religion, sex (including pregnancy, sexual orientation, or gender identity), national origin, age (40 or older), disability (which can be broadly interpreted) and genetic information (including family medical history).[70] People who report or threaten to report discrimination are also protected.

Discrimination

Most employees who are fired will consider themselves to have been discrimination victims. Their possibly flawed logic is that they got fired, while five of their co-workers did not, so therefore it "must" be discrimination.

You can expect that, at a minimum, any terminated employee will be looking carefully to see whether they can make a case for being in one of the protected classes of employees and that any employee who expects to be fired imminently will consider quickly making a complaint to someone official to gain protection for themselves as whistleblowers.

---

[70] https://www.eeoc.gov/employers/small-business/3-who-protected-employment-discrimination retrieved August 13, 2020

Basis for Termination

The best advice I can give is to forget that Employment at Will even exists and to ensure that you can show good reasons for every termination.

On this basis, there are really two categories of termination. The first category is performance-based termination. Termination for substandard performance should be done gradually. You may have heard the phrase "progressive discipline," which is the appropriate way to handle an underperforming employee.

Progressive discipline means that the employee is counseled after the first transgression, counseled again after the second deviation (and warned that any further shortfalls will result in termination), and then let go on the third inappropriate action. Contrary to what many dentists believe, progressive discipline does <u>not</u> require the actions for which each warning was issued to be similar or identical. So, an employee can receive their initial warning for arriving late for work, their second warning for not conforming to the office dress code and be terminated for not closing the day correctly in practice management software.

What makes applying progressive discipline much easier is to have a fully developed system in your practice for HR management. This system includes a policy manual, meaningful job descriptions, performing regular (and honest) performance reviews, and quickly, decisively, and consistently dealing with performance lapses across all employees. In the example, I used about the three transgressions that resulted in an employee being terminated, the best position you can be in as an employer is to have clearly articulated policies for tardiness, dress code, and front-office procedures.

Applying your rules inconsistently quickly gives an employee a basis for making a discrimination argument. So, if one employee is counseled or terminated for behavior accepted when done by other employees, you are begging to be on the wrong end of a discrimination claim. Consider a situation where you have different but undocumented expectations of how clinical and front-desk staff should dress. The receptionist who shows up wearing scrubs and gets counseled for not wearing business attire may feel that they are being discriminated against.

As I mentioned, the exact timing of termination should never be known by an employee in advance to avoid anticipatory actions. Still, an underperforming employee should understand he or she is not meeting your expectations.

Firing for Lack of Integrity

The second category of termination is integrity-based. This category is sometimes referred to as termination for "just cause." Dishonesty, including embezzlement, is a clear case of an integrity violation, as are the "three Is" - insolence, insubordination, and intoxication.

Although termination for just cause does give you the ability to terminate immediately, I usually recommend a slightly different approach. We often suggest that the offending employee be suspended immediately and without pay, with termination normally following, typically two or three days later. Your immediate need with an employee who has done something wrong is to separate the employee from the practice and suspending them accomplishes that. Suspending also prevents what I think is the worst thing you can do when terminating an employee, firing someone when you are angry. Firing when upset is when steps get skipped or forgotten, and things get said that can bite you in a sensitive part of your anatomy. Suspending gives you the time you need to lock down your practice properly, attend to details like separation paperwork and the employee's final paycheck, and get your emotions under control.

Suspending before termination also allows you to give the employee a chance to bring forward whatever exculpatory or mitigating information they wish to. Sometimes this is an explanation that prevents you from making a big mistake, and sometimes it is a confession that facilitates investigation and prosecution. Whether anything useful comes from the employee or not, it is never a bad idea to give them a chance, and the time, to explain their conduct before taking the irreversible step of firing them. If the employee subsequently sues you for wrongful termination, you will be glad that you offered them a chance to make an explanation.

Can I Search an Employee's Workspace?

To answer a question that we are frequently asked, "their" desk, workspace, and computer are really yours. The Fourth Amendment protects against "unreasonable" search and seizure, but this limits government agencies' ability, not that of employers. Workplace searches, with a sufficient basis, are normally reasonable.

While this statement is not a substitute for situation-specific advice, in a situation where you suspect wrongdoing, you generally have the right to search a desk, computer, workspace, or locker owned by your practice without giving prior notice to or having the consent of, the affected employee.[71] This ability does not normally extend to personally-owned items like briefcases, purses, or personally-owned electronic devices.

Some employers do include in their employment terms a provision to the effect that personally owned electronic devices, if brought on to the business' premises, are subject to search. Since I'm not an employment law expert, I can't express an opinion on the enforceability of such a term. Still, I also can't see a downside to including such a term in your employment policy.

How to Fire

Prosperident has developed a termination checklist that covers many steps to be taken in the event of a termination. Annex A has a checklist of important things to take care of when terminating an employee. If you prefer an electronic copy of this checklist, please email us at requests@prosperident.com, and we will be happy to supply one.

The following list should be used to supplement the advice you get from an HR expert on handling an employee's termination. This guidance is based on what is "humane" for the

---

[71]   "Workplace Searches and Interrogations." Findlaw. Accessed January 17, 2020. https://employment.findlaw.com/workplace-privacy/workplace-searches-and-interrogations.html.

fired employee and that when terminating an employee who has been stealing, I understand that you may not have a strong urge to protect their dignity. However, regardless of what they have done, putting them in a situation where they might harm themselves because you mishandled their termination is not something you want on your conscience. At the same time, you also need to protect your practice against someone who may try to destroy embezzlement evidence or retaliate against you.

When firing someone, the following are some guidelines that will protect both you and the terminated employee:

1. The reason for termination needs to be worked out with your HR advisors. We encourage the use of something that is non-accusatory. For example, it would be better to say that "money is missing that was under your custody" or that the employee "failed to identify and report out-of-balance situations as required" than the more inflammatory "embezzlement." In this area, good job descriptions that spell out responsibilities and accountabilities are definitely your friends; it is hard to terminate someone for not doing their job when that job is not clearly spelled out.

2. Consider using the "suspension-termination" technique that We discussed previously. In a suspension-termination, the employee receives a letter outlining the discrepancy found, puts them on immediate suspension, and informs them that, unless a satisfactory explanation is provided within 48 hours, the employee will be terminated without further notice.

3. Keep all oral and written communication with the employee businesslike. The employee can be expected to try to appeal to your emotions at some point in this process, and you should not indicate that you are open to this.

4. As I mentioned, do not "fire when angry."

5. If possible, avoid letting someone go at the end of the week. An early or mid-week termination allows the ex-employee to busy themselves with looking for another job. In contrast, termination at the end of the week enables them to "stew" over the weekend, which is not always a good idea. The Journal of Emergency Medicine reports that Sundays and Mondays are the peak days for suicides,[72] so to avoid this and any mischief they might create; we recommend avoiding termination on a Thursday or Friday.

6. It is better to let someone go at the end of the day. This step avoids making them do the "walk of shame" where they pack their possessions in front of their coworkers. For the fired employee, this is a humiliating experience that can usually be avoided with proper planning.

7. An exit interview should be carefully planned, and normally your words should be scripted in advance. It is a good idea to have a second person in the room to act as a witness.

---

[72] https://www.sciencemag.org/news/2014/04/suicide-most-common-two-days-week retrieved August 12, 2020.

8. When terminating for wrongdoing, the most productive question is along the lines of "I'm not asking you if you did it; I know that you did. What I want to know is why you did it. This query often shifts the conversation from an unproductive cycle of accusation and denial to the employee defending or rationalizing their actions.

9. Be prepared in case the employee indicates a desire to make a confession. Full details on obtaining a confession from an employee are in Chapter 28.

10. Once you tell someone that their job with you has ended, they should not be left unsupervised, even for a minute, while on your premises.

11. Have a box ready for them to pack their possessions.

12. Do not allow them to touch any computer or the phone system once they have been told they are fired. If this person claims to have personal information on a work computer, instruct them to note the files' location on a piece of paper and let them know that you will arrange to have their personal information transferred to a flash drive by your IT advisors.

13. Closely supervise the removal of any paper to ensure that what they are taking is, in fact, personal and not a patient list or other information that belongs to the practice. Suppose there are items where there is a disagreement between the parties on whether it is personal or belongs to the practice. In that case, one option is to put the disputed material in a box or envelope, seal it, and keep it until the question can be resolved.

14. Ask the fired employee (preferably more than once) if they have a safe way home. Offer to pay for a ride if they would otherwise be taking public transit or are driving their own car home (which might be unsafe if they are upset). Do not, under any circumstance, drive them home yourself.

15. Disable their user accounts in practice management software and ensure that any remote access they might have to your network is removed. If you are in any doubt and your IT consultant is not available, **unplug your router** to disconnect your system from the internet until the security of your network can be confirmed.

16. Remove their alarm access code and **change the locks** to your practice. Getting a key back from someone does not mean that it is the only key in their possession, and the words "DO NOT DUPLICATE" on the side of a key will not reliably stop that key from being copied. The only way to gain physical security is to change the locks. Also, arrange to have the employee's alarm code removed immediately from the alarm system. Now is probably a good time to remind you that it is a terrible idea to have a single alarm code used by everybody. If this is your practice, when you fire someone, all remaining team members are forced to learn a new code, and it is so tempting to convince yourself that it is fine just to continue using the current "unicode," even if the fired employee still has it.

Following these steps and the guidance you receive from your HR advisor will help ensure that your termination goes smoothly and with minimal risk to your practice.

References and Defamation

I'll address one issue that many people misunderstand about giving (and receiving) references about employees. Most of us have heard something along the lines of "you can't say anything bad about a former employee" or "you can't say anything at all."

Neither of these statements is accurate. The concern is that you commit something called "defamation." Defamation can take two forms; libel (written defamation) and slander, which is spoken defamation.

To constitute defamation, a statement must have <u>all</u> the following characteristics:

1. It must be a false statement of fact. So, if a statement is true or not a factual matter, it can never be defamatory. For example, saying that under no circumstance would you ever rehire a specific employee is not defamatory because it is a statement of what you plan to do in the future and is, therefore, not a factual statement.
2. It must be "published," which, in this sense, means that the statement must be made to a third party. Telling an employee something in private about their performance cannot be defamation no matter what is said.
3. The person making the statement must have known, or could reasonably be expected to have known, that the statement was false.
4. The statement was not the subject of privilege. We are all familiar with the attorney-client privilege

concept that allows us to have candid conversations with an attorney representing us. What many practice owners do not realize is that, in many states, there is a similar provision for conversations with a prospective employer. Twenty states give "qualified privilege" to information provided by a current or former employer to a prospective employer. In these states, truthful communications about a current or former employee's job performance or employment qualifications are privileged if a communication is based on credible evidence and made without malice. A privileged comment cannot form the basis of a defamation claim.

5. The person about whom the statement was made suffered harm because of the statement.

So contrary to belief, you are within your legal rights to make truthful, non-malicious statements to someone calling you and asking for a reference.

That doesn't always make doing so a good idea. Negative information that you pass to a prospective employer has a good chance of getting back to your former employee. Since this information is often being passed orally between several parties, just like the children's game Telephone, it is likely that what gets back to the employee is slightly different than what you actually said.

Former employees are often willing to sue you. Even if they have little chance of winning in court, being sued is a nuisance. Some lawyers are happy to take on a case against a dentist on a contingency fee basis hoping for a quick settlement and an easy payday.

Suppose your ex-employee has found a contingency-fee lawyer. In that case, your ex-employee can be in the position of not being out-of-pocket for legal fees while you are paying your attorney on an hourly basis, so doing anything that might prompt a lawsuit is to be avoided.

Giving a Negative Reference

When providing a job reference on an unsatisfactory employee, my suggestion is to confirm employment dates and job title on leaving and limiting your other comments to stating emphatically that there is no possibility whatsoever that the employee will be rehired. This declaration conveys the impression to their next prospective employer that something bad happened while giving nothing of substance for an "ambulance chasing" attorney to get their teeth into. Following this practice rigorously and keeping good notes about calls received from prospective employers will also stand you in good stead if there is ever a question about what was said in a conversation about an ex-employee.

Obviously, these techniques will not ward off every lawsuit from a disgruntled former employee, but they are preferable to creating a more complex basis for a claim against you.

25

Delegation vs. Abdication

Delegation is essential to the financial well-being of a practice. The existence of well-trained clinical and administrative staff allows a practice's doctors to focus on their unique (and high value) competencies.

The concept of clinical delegation is well-understood by dentists and is first encountered in dental school.

However, the delegation of the administrative functions in a practice is normally experienced much later when a dentist becomes a practice owner. It happens without the dentist having the benefit of any training.

Compounding the lack of training on how to delegate administrative responsibilities effectively is that most dentists benchmark themselves by how their practice performs clinically and take no comparable pleasure from having a smoothly administered practice.

The combination of lack of training and low level of interest often creates a "perfect storm" where dentists unconsciously fall into the trap of turning **delegation**, which is desirable and beneficial, into **abdication**, which can be dangerous.

So, what is the difference between these two concepts? It can be summarized as follows:

Delegation is the devolution of tasks or responsibilities, but with accountability to the practice owner. Abdication is the offloading of responsibility, but with no corresponding answerability. It may also involve a lack of transparency and a lack of skepticism or independent verification.

In a clinical setting, accountability is clearly understood by dentists. You have ownership of, for example, a poor impression taken by a dental assistant, and you have a clear responsibility to ensure that clinical staff has suitable training in CPR to be prepared to handle medical emergencies.

Clinical accountability is aided by the regulated nature of dentistry, dental assisting, and dental hygiene, where members of these professions are trained, tested, certified, and normally required to maintain their competency through continuing education. Also, the dentist's knowledge of the work carried on by clinical team members is normally high.

In contrast, there is no required certification to be a receptionist, financial coordinator, or office manager. Most people in these positions have received their training on the job with you or while working at another dental practice. While there is considerable information and training available to people in administrative positions, it isn't mandatory or comprehensive. And to make matters worse, unlike the clinical situation, the doctor is usually less knowledgeable about what goes on in the administration of his or her practice than the people who hold jobs in that area, limiting the dentist's ability to train and effectively supervise front desk staff.

It's a recipe for disaster. You are asked to oversee people who often have little formal training in their jobs without your having the benefit of either detailed knowledge or any idea of how to exercise oversight. Furthermore, if you are like most dentists, keeping an eye on your front desk isn't a responsibility that you enjoy in any case. So, it doesn't take much to convince you just to step away from what goes on there (i.e., abdication).

What should a dentist do to increase accountability? Here are some ideas:

1. Remember that accountability is more than an abstract concept. There is a tendency to believe that, because you sign someone's paycheck, they are accountable to you. Conceptually this is true, but you derive no benefit from this relationship unless it translates into actual oversight. Unless you are involved and asking questions, you have abdicated.

2. Effective oversight requires knowledge. Administration is not a cruel joke that the world has played on the dental profession; it is a vital link in the chain between the treatment of patients and your financial well-being. Learn to do the basics in your practice management software — enter treatment, print reports, and process a payment. In addition to gaining familiarity with your software, learn to do your office manager's

key functions. Learn what the most important reports from your practice management software are and what they mean.

3. Be the boss. This responsibility does not mean that you need to be "bossy," but it does require you to make some rules and stick to them. Here are three rules that every practice should have:

   o Documentation of activity. Every administrative person needs to document what they do and how they do it. If they become ill, retire, or move away, their "institutional knowledge" shouldn't disappear with them. This approach requires a detailed job description (not the kind used when hiring) plus some backup information (references to the manual for your practice management software, etc.) These "position guidebooks" should be consolidated with each of you and your office manager keeping a copy.

   o Cross-training — This is closely aligned with the previous point and is intended to ensure that your practice doesn't grind to a halt because of the unplanned absence of one person. You should be one of the people cross-trained in your office manager's duties.

   o Mandatory vacations for all staff. The best way to test your cross-training is to put it to use. Make every employee take at least two consecutive weeks off each year when the office is functioning (times when the office is completely shut down do not count — the real point is to have someone else filling in for the employee). In addition to ensuring a distribution of your institutional knowledge, having other people temporarily fill administrative jobs provides one of the best chances of catching embezzlement.

4. Trust, but verify. There are a few things that every practice owner needs to do to ensure that their practice records have integrity:

   o First, you need to review day-end information from your practice every day to ensure that your work was accurately recorded and to be alert for suspicious transactions.

   o Verify that the correct amount of money was deposited in your bank account. This verification should include both the "physical" deposit (cash and checks) and amounts deposited electronically (usually checks and electronic funds transfers). Normally, this necessitates waiting a few days for delayed amounts such as credit card payments to reach your bank. Verification should be done via electronic banking; a deposit slip is not sufficient. I have a lot more to say about oversight in Chapter 17.

   o It is important to ensure that your daily reports "articulate" with month-end reports. This articulation ensures that there is no after-hours activity in your software hidden from you. We have developed a spreadsheet that does the heavy lifting for you.

While the process of managing the activities of your practice's front-office staff can seem daunting at first, the basic steps outlined here will give you a great start.

26

The Question of "Trust"

I had an interesting discussion a while ago with a learned (and outspoken) dentist friend. The topic was the possibility of a spouse embezzling from a dentist. We discussed the possibility of spousal embezzlement in Chapter 7.

My friend lives in the "real world" and acknowledged the possibility but found the topic uncomfortable and probably self-fulfilling. My friend's view was that if he failed to trust his spouse, he would be making embezzlement, and its usual companion when spouses embezzle, divorce, more likely.

The conversation made my mind turn to the interesting way that we humans deal with trust. To us, trust is binary. We view someone as either "trustworthy" or not. We also have a positive bias; we want to trust people. We also prefer to get the trust question out of the way early in our relationship with a person.

So, we assume that certain people are "above suspicion." I can always surprise an audience of dentists when I show them examples of where:

- Dentists were stealing from each other in group practices, which We discussed in Chapter 8.
- Spouses were embezzling from dentists.
- Children were embezzling from a parent's dental practice where they work.[73]

Similarly, an overt display of strong religious beliefs will not stop people from embezzling. Our investigators regularly see people who are highly involved in a religious community convicted of embezzlement.[74]

Recent research by psychologists on the behavioral characteristics of trustworthy people suggests that "guilt-proneness" predicts trustworthiness better than other personality measures; people prone to guilt are far more likely to be trustworthy.[75]

---

[73] For an example, see the story of how someone received an 18-month prison sentence for embezzling from her father's practice -- https://www.prosperident.com/dont-see-one-every-day-receptionist-accused-embezzling-fathers-practice/

[74] See for example a pillar of the 7th Day Adventist Community convicted of stealing $800,000 from a dental practice -- https://www.prosperident.com/walla-walla-educator-bookkeeper-7th-day-adventist-embezzles-823k-sentenced-18-months-prison/

[75] Levine, E. E., Bitterly, T. B., Cohen, T. R., & Schweitzer, M. E. (2018). Who is trustworthy? Predicting trustworthy intentions and behavior. *Journal of Personality and Social Psychology, 115*(3), 468-494. doi:10.1037/pspi0000136

Are most people dishonest? Of course not. But we need to address our very human desires to give people the benefit of the doubt, consider people trustworthy because of some personal characteristic they have, or trust them forever based on a judgment that we made early in the relationship.

As discussed in Chapter 4, ultimately, almost anyone can find themselves in a situation where their ethical foundations may be tested. The concept of trustworthiness is essentially a gauge of how severe the pressure must be to cause someone to break their own rules. Clearly, some people will abandon their beliefs more easily than others, but pragmatically, we should assume that ultimately anybody, given sufficient external pressure, can commit a dishonest act.

For this reason, we need to be mindful that trustworthiness is a concept that has some fluidity and thus needs to be re-evaluated periodically. Reexamining the appropriate level of trust to give someone is not a concept that comes naturally to most, so some mindfulness is normally required.

27

What You Must Do If You Suspect Embezzlement

In a situation where embezzlement is suspected, a misstep can make your problems far worse than they already are. Unfortunately, this is one of those situations where following your instinct can often steer you in the wrong direction. Please note that this discussion applies to instances where embezzlement is suspected but not yet confirmed; I will talk about what steps to take when embezzlement is definite in Chapter 28.

Annex B is what we refer to as the Panic List. This list condenses the important dos and don'ts into a couple of pages.

The biggest mistake that dentists make is that they do something that alerts the suspected thief that they are under suspicion.

First, there is always the possibility that your suspicion is misplaced. It could be that embezzlement is not taking place at all, or it is happening, but the thief has been misidentified. In either of these situations, telegraphing your concerns to the person you suspect (which amounts to telling an innocent person that you question their integrity) will irreparably damage the working relationship. It might even expose you to a lawsuit.

On the other hand, if embezzlement occurs, and you have correctly identified the embezzler, making them aware of your suspicions prematurely can be outright dangerous.

When an embezzler thinks that he or she is about to be discovered (and possibly go to jail, have their friends read about them in the newspaper, have their spouse find out about their illegal activities, etc.), their thoughts turn to self-preservation. The desire to protect oneself is compelling, and anyone who has ever taken lifeguard training is aware of the danger of getting too close to someone who believes that they are in danger of drowning.

My team and I have seen instances of destroyed hard drives, missing backup media, and in a couple of extreme cases, arson and even murder committed by dental office embezzlers attempting to avoid the consequences of their actions.

Although such efforts usually end badly for the embezzler, the dangers they pose for the involved dentists are considerable.

I see many dentists going to Facebook groups or Dentaltown to get some help from peers on what to do next. Much of the advice that is given is provided with the best of intentions but is dead wrong. Here is one example that a member of our team spotted in a Facebook group. There is so much wrong with this statement!

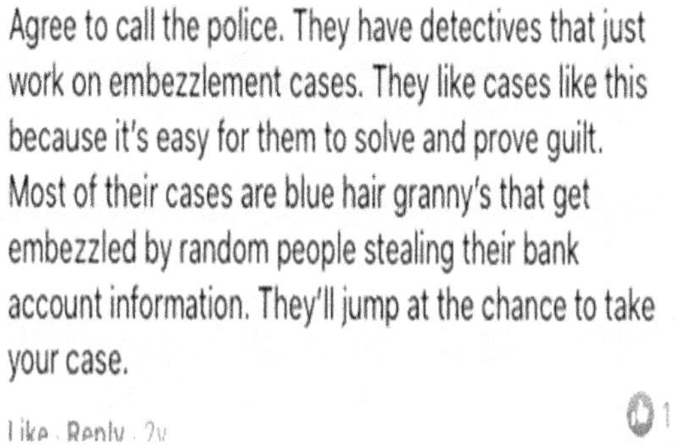

> Agree to call the police. They have detectives that just work on embezzlement cases. They like cases like this because it's easy for them to solve and prove guilt. Most of their cases are blue hair granny's that get embezzled by random people stealing their bank account information. They'll jump at the chance to take your case.
>
> Like . Reply . 2v

Figure 7 – Misguided advice from Facebook.

First, the police categorically do not have any expertise in this issue. As discussed later in this chapter, these crimes are complex and require knowledge beyond what any police department possesses. They know that the prosecution of embezzlement cases, even if they have help from experts like us, takes years and in certain cases has a low probability of success, so they are often far from enthusiastic when a case comes their way, particularly if it is evident that not enough work has been done to assemble the evidence properly. So pretty much everything this well-intended poster says is off the mark. And this happens a lot. I see dentists express embezzlement concerns all the time on social media, and some outrageously incorrect advice dispensed freely. When I can, I step in to set the record straight, but it can be a hugely frustrating exercise to watch some of these train wrecks.

Here are some actions to avoid at this critical juncture:

- Questioning or confronting the suspect. Questioning a suspect is only meaningful when you know a lot more than you presumably do at this point. If you confront someone when you have only unconfirmed suspicions, the limits of your knowledge will be very evident to them, which means that they will assertively deny stealing from you. You will have exposed the cards in your hand and gained nothing in exchange.
- Calling the police. Embezzlement, particularly in a dental practice, is a highly technical crime and significantly different than most of the crimes police investigate. In most police matters, determining **what** was stolen is the easy part, and the challenge is to find **who** did it. In contrast, when embezzlement is committed, the question of who is relatively simple – there usually is a handful of suspects. The real challenge is to determine what was taken.

No law enforcement agency is appropriately equipped to perform a primary investigation of embezzlement in your practice. Typically, they are quite capable of performing a secondary investigation (where they do things like obtain banking records for a suspect and compare spending patterns of the suspect to income), but to be able to understand and analyze transactions in your practice management software requires several skills that police do not possess.

Additionally, the police do not view their role as determining what was stolen; it is the victim's responsibility to figure that part out. The police's job is to ensure that the law is applied correctly based on what was taken from you. And they must do this with limited budgets and a crushing workload.

- Starting a claim with the insurance company that covers you for employee dishonesty. It is fine to contact your insurance company to determine your coverage limit, but when you make such a call, the question the insurance company will ask you next is whether you wish to open a claim. The person speaking with you may point to a speedier resolution if you get started now but opening a claim at this juncture is not a good idea. You are not yet able to answer the most basic questions needed to move your claim ahead, such as how much money you lost, but opening the claim usually has an undesirable side effect. Most insurance contracts have limitation periods that allow you a specified period (six months is typical) to bring a claim forward. This clock starts at the time of discovery. So, if you are at the point where you suspect but have not yet confirmed the embezzlement, insurance companies will treat the time when you opened your claim as the moment of discovery. So, by starting a claim, effectively, you start a clock ticking and effectively shorten the window in which you can claim your loss.

- Engaging "dabblers" to assist you. I have seen dentists with embezzlement concerns turn to many different people for assistance. Software trainers, practice management consultants, the manager of another dental office, the practice's IT person, the practice's CPA, or generalist forensic investigators are some of the people to whom some desperate dentists reach out. Except for the final group, none of these people are trained as investigators, which means that there is a good possibility of them trampling over evidence and having insufficient qualifications and credibility to provide an expert loss report or expert testimony in court. The non-dental forensic investigators face a steep learning curve to acquire the dental knowledge they need. They will usually bill you for the time they spend learning enough about dentistry to perform their work.

Unfortunately, these well-intended people are unaware of the intricacies of this kind of work, or perhaps their desire to generate a fee draws them beyond their area of expertise, so they may agree to take on work that they probably should not. Using people who are not real experts can be expected to increase your final cost, delay the ultimate resolution of the issue, and possibly allow a thief to walk away or expose you to a lawsuit. Just as your profession has its specialists, so does ours.

- Engaging your attorney to quarterback the process. While your attorney can provide value in some limited areas, such as terminating a staff member or commencing a lawsuit against a thief, they are not investigators, and they often lack understanding of the investigative process. Having your attorney act as the "project manager" for an investigation can drastically slow the investigation process and increase your costs. It is entirely okay to inform your attorney about the issue you are facing. Still, you should be aware of the limits to the value that their attempt to participate in the investigation process actively will add.

- Failing to recognize conflicts of interest. A few people may want to be involved in the investigation process who may have divided loyalties. Your accountant may believe that eventually, the finger of blame may be pointed at him or her for not detecting the embezzlement. As discussed in Chapter 14, in general, accountants have minimal opportunity to discover dental practice embezzlement, but a concern that the accountant may shoulder some of the blame for not detecting the embezzlement sooner may cause the accountant's interest to be conflicted. There is also your insurance company, who may offer to engage an investigator to assist with your claim. An insurance company investigator will likely not have specific dental expertise, and their mandate is usually limited to investigating only to the point of the coverage limit of your insurance. Suppose your coverage is $25,000, which is the typical amount carried by dental practices. In that case, an insurance-appointed investigator will have no interest in determining the total loss you experienced or in uncovering the full spectrum of methodologies employed by your thief.

- Acting unnaturally, in whatever form this takes. Inappropriate or telling actions often include asking for several reports from your practice management software that you have never requested before or spending long periods in your office with the door closed talking to your CPA on the phone or making sudden changes to office routines or access within your practice management software. If a team member is stealing from you, they ask themselves daily whether you are on the cusp of discovering their activity. Your acting differently or changing things in any way may convince them to do something drastic to protect their liberty.

A few months ago, I got a call from a dentist who had concerns about a couple of team members. The dentist proudly told me how, before she called us, she had gone into her practice management software and reduced the privileges of the people in question. This dentist was surprised when I instructed her to immediately drive back to the office to undo the changes she had made so that nothing would appear to have changed the next morning. I explained to the doctor that the amount likely to be stolen until we progressed far enough into our investigation to confirm her suspicions was far less than the potential damage that could befall her practice from her premature disclosure to the suspects that she was onto them.

If you have suspicions, you need expert guidance, and quickly. Do not waste your time and money on the services offered by well-intended, non-experts, or "dabblers."

My team and I are always happy to have a conversation with a practice owner who suspects embezzlement. Please feel free to reach out to us through our website or by calling 888-398-2327.

The cost of inaction

Several years ago, I got a call from a dentist. As this dentist described his situation, it became clear that embezzlement was very likely happening, given the suspect's behavior. We were retained and began our intake process. The dentist contacted us two days later to say that he was discontinuing the investigation, and the reason was that there was a labor shortage in the area of the practice. In other words, it was better to keep an employee who was stealing from the dentist than trying to find another staff member in an area with few available replacements. I could not believe my ears.

A few days later, I got a call from another dentist. One of this dentist's staff had taken the scrap gold in the office, sold it, and kept the proceeds. The question that this dentist was calling to ask me was whether the employee should be fired. While the amount involved was small, the answer to this question seemed so obvious that I am still having trouble believing that it was asked.

What concerned me about both incidents is the dentists' apparent willingness to accept some level of dishonesty from their employees.

Simply put, there should be ZERO tolerance for dishonest acts from your team members. Someone willing to sell a few hundred dollars of your gold has already crossed the ethical hurdle that employees must transcend before they steal anything and everything from you and your practice. It is only a matter of time before their actions evolve into a more direct and monetarily significant form of stealing. And the dentist who suddenly decided that a local labor shortage existed had bought into the idea that the suspect is entirely indispensable to the practice.

The costs of inaction can include severe financial damage, and it also consigns dentists to long-term uncertainty. Always having to wonder what these employees are "up to" will continue for as long as they work in these practices.

"If They Aren't Stealing, How Do You Like Them as an Employee"?

When I get calls from a dentist who isn't sure if an employee is stealing, this is often a question that I ask. The responses tend to be polarized – either this is an otherwise ideal employee or a mediocre one.

When I ask this question, and the response is that the employee is sub-par, I often suggest termination now. If this person will be fired if they aren't stealing (and they will certainly be fired if they do have their hand in your pocket), then the best course of action is to let them go now.

Firing them now lifts a weight off the doctor's shoulders. The practice owner no longer needs to face the employee daily and pretend that everything is fine while simultaneously wondering how much that person is stealing today.

The exception to this advice occurs when this employee, due to age or other factors, cannot be terminated without consequences, in which case confirming embezzlement will eliminate any potential wrongful termination issues. A full discussion of termination is in Chapter 24.

28

Your Course of Action if Embezzlement Has Already Been Confirmed

The path is a bit clearer if embezzlement has already been confirmed, either by you or by your investigator. If the embezzler is still working for you, the first obvious step is to fire the thief. It is an excellent idea to obtain some HR assistance in ensuring that this is done correctly; this advice could come from your attorney if he or she has that expertise or from one of the dental-specific HR firms.

Please see Chapter 24 for our guidance on termination, which is not a substitute for knowledgeable HR advice.

Along the lines discussed in Chapter 27, if an embezzler is not yet aware that you are on to them, please keep it that way until you are fully prepared to face them.

Annex B contains our Panic List of immediate dos and don'ts when you have a potential embezzlement issue.

Should I bother?

The next decision you must make is whether to investigate. It is tempting to assume that, once you no longer employ the staff member, the logical course of action is to "walk away" and not bother to have an investigation conducted. The 2019 CDP Survey determined that 22% of the embezzlements that were reported were not investigated.[76] Generally, not investigating is a mistake. As tempting as it is just to walk away, there are several consequences to not finding out what happened:

1. You are forgoing any chance of financial recovery. Most practices have at least some insurance coverage for this, which will generally pay more than the cost of an investigation. There are also other possible recovery sources, so normally, an investigation is a "cash-positive" activity.
2. When a thief confesses, it is likely to be far less than the whole truth. Esteemed fraud investigator Chris Marquet estimates that, on average, when thieves confess, they admit to stealing between one quarter and one half of what they have taken.[77] In my own experience, the percentage confessed to is lower. Thieves tend to base their confessions on what they think you will believe. In

---

[76] American Dental Association. (2019). 2018 CDP Survey on Employee Theft in the Dental Practice. *Center for Dental Practice*

[77] Marquet, Chris T. *The 2013 Marquet Report on Embezzlement*. Marquet International, Ltd., 19 Dec. 2013, mediad.publicbroadcasting.net/p/vpr/files/The_2013_Marquet_Report_On_Embezzlement.pdf.

many cases, they have (probably willfully) lost track of how much they have stolen. Whatever the reasons, a confession normally significantly understates the actual problem.

3. Most thieves employ multiple methods of stealing. So, the discovery of one modality does not mean that you fully understand what happened. There is likely more stealing, and the investigation needs to be broader than merely finding more occurrences of the methodology that has already emerged.

4. There are two ways for an embezzler to steal — many embezzlers steal from you; lots also use your practice as a platform to steal from insurance companies. While you are within your rights to decide to walk away from the former, failing to identify and address money stolen from insurance companies (stolen using your name) tends to migrate you in the eyes of the insurance companies from co-victim to perpetrator. And I probably do not need to explain why having a large company with deep pockets and little tolerance for fraud angry with you is a bad idea.

5. A frequent consequence of embezzlement is adulterated records in your practice. Your practice management software may show balances owed by patients that aren't real, or clinical records may have been altered while committing the embezzlement. Identifying what has actually happened is an important part of understanding the impact on your financial and clinical records.

6. Something that surprises many practice owners is that embezzlement takes a considerable amount of work on the part of a thief. The hours they spend stealing from you get covered in one of two ways; either they spend extra time at work, or if it is not possible or something that the thief does not want to do, they neglect some of their primary job functions.

7. Whatever weaknesses in your systems were exploited by the embezzler still exist and are available to the next larcenous employee. By not having an investigation, you lose the chance to learn from being embezzled.

8. While the lessons learned may be painful, this is one of your best chances to gain some knowledge that will benefit you for the rest of your career. The 2019 CDP Survey showed that 46% of embezzlement victims were destined to be victimized again.[78]

9. You can take comfort that you are protecting one, and possibly several, of your peers from experiencing the same grief you have.

Thieves Who Want to Confess

Sometimes, an embezzler will want to make a confession when they realize that they are about to get caught. Possibly this is because the thief feels guilty about what they have done,

---

[78]   American Dental Association. (2019). 2018 CDP Survey on Employee Theft in the Dental Practice. *Center for Dental Practice*

and they wish to unburden themselves. In other cases, the thief believes that the punishment they will receive may be reduced if they "come clean."

As previously mentioned, most confessions understate the amount stolen. Here are some guidelines to deal with a thief who wants to give a confession.

First, and most importantly, **let them do it.** A properly obtained confession is of enormous value in getting a conviction for an embezzler. Also, there is often information provided by the confessor that will assist tremendously in an investigation.

Next, insist that, if someone wants to confess, they do so **in writing**. A verbal confession's evidentiary value is minimal.

Here are some guidelines on obtaining a written confession:

1. A confession statement must be VOLUNTARY. Coerced statements are not admissible. It is fine to suggest to an embezzler that it might be in their best interest to make a confession (which many embezzlers want to do anyway). Still, embezzlers should not be offered some form of reward if they confess or be threatened with punishment if they do not. The first paragraph of a confession statement should confirm that it is made voluntarily.

2. Similarly, it is important when meeting with a suspect that you give no perception that their freedom to walk out of the interview is in any way impaired. Locking the door to the room where you are meeting with a suspect,

3. It is essential to document in their confession that the embezzler knew that what he or she did was wrong.

4. It is also valuable to document some elements of the embezzler's activities to conceal their embezzlement. Documenting concealment cements the argument that the crime committed was one of premeditation and not impulse.
5. One witness's signature (which can be you) is required by law, but having two witnesses attesting is preferred.
6. If the statement extends over more than one page, the embezzler and each witness should initial each page except the last page, which will have the signatures, so it does not need initials.
7. The "Miranda" warning that most of us have seen administered on a TV show applies only when someone is being questioned by law enforcement. There is no comparable requirement for you to administer such a warning.
8. Remember that thieves typically confess to far less than they actually stole.

Contents of a Confession

The statement should contain the following:

1. Voluntariness of confession.
2. The embezzler's intent. That is to say that they knew their conduct was wrong.
3. The approximate date(s) of the offense(s).
4. The approximate dollar amount of losses. This amount is the embezzler's estimate, not yours!

5. An estimated number of instances of embezzlement.
6. If embezzlement stopped, when and why (i.e., the embezzlement stopped when the embezzler was fired).
7. Moral justification. That is any statement the embezzler makes justifying his or her actions.
8. Truthfulness. The confession statement should explicitly mention that the statement being made is true.

Financial Recovery

Almost every dentist who has been stolen from gets some recovery, and a lucky few get it all back. So, how do you get your money back if you have been a victim? I am glad you asked! The following are your best bets for recovering your losses.

Insurance

Many dentists do not realize that they have insurance for employee dishonesty. As previously mentioned, this coverage is part of your property insurance. The typical amount of coverage that my team encounters is $25,000, although some dentists have only $10,000 in insurance for employee dishonesty, and a few practices have higher coverage levels.

Based on what you now know about the kind of losses that dentists experience from theft, you are undoubtedly aware that neither of these amounts is likely to be adequate if you suffer embezzlement. One of my recommendations is to contact the agent who provides your property insurance to explore the possibility of increasing this coverage. Most insurance companies will happily increase this coverage to $75,000, and the increased premium cost is quite modest, so I encourage this. The insurance company will most likely ask for your certification that you are not currently aware of any potential claims. If you are already concerned about a staff member, it is probably too late to increase your current coverage.

Getting paid from your insurance company is usually the easiest money for you to recover. At the appropriate time, you will open a claim and provide the insurance company with the loss report that your investigator has provided to you. Insurance companies invariably require you to have made a police report as a precondition for making a claim. Reporting to the police is a general requirement for all theft claims and is not specific to embezzlement. Once the insurance company's paperwork is complete, and after a short processing interval, you should receive your check. The only instance where you will run into a problem is if your report was done by someone with insufficient professional qualifications or experience or is otherwise lacking somehow. In this case, the insurance company may ask some questions or engage its own forensic investigator to review the report or even perform a separate investigation. Fortunately, it is rare for our clients that, when Prosperident is involved, we get more than a cursory question or two from the practice's insurance company.

Many dentists do not realize that it is not necessary to obtain a conviction or even to establish who took the money for the purpose of claiming your insurance. For insurance purposes, the need is only to establish that it was stolen.

One other question that arises is what happens if you receive funds from your insurance company, and there is also some recovery from the embezzler. Does your insurance company get this money, or does it go to you?

Other Recovery Sources

Collecting your insurance benefit is a relatively simple matter. It is time to look at the other, less attractive, possibilities for recovery.

If someone has stolen by hijacking checks payable to you or your practice, you can recover from the bank that allowed someone to cash or deposit your checks through an indirect route. This recovery is discussed in more detail in a subsequent section of this chapter. Obviously, this pathway is only available if a certain pattern of theft was used. My team and I see theft of checks in a sizeable portion of our cases, and significant recovery is normally possible for these victims.

If you are a victim of a "mixed" theft involving the theft of both checks and cash or some other asset, it is important to claim your losses strategically. With a finite amount of insurance coverage, you normally want to preserve your insurance coverage to use against cash losses and not "spend" it against losses from stolen checks, for which you have other recovery options.

Once insurance and third-party recovery from stolen checks have been addressed, if there is a loss remaining, the next consideration is whether the thief has any ability to repay the money that they stole.

It probably will not surprise you to hear that it is rare to recover large up-front amounts from thieves; most of them are at least as good at spending as they are at stealing. In the case of Needy thieves, they are stealing to address an imbalance in household finances, so stolen money has usually disappeared into groceries and rent. The Greedy thieves who steal for ego spend money conspicuously, most often in ways that do not produce enduring value. Happily, there are exceptions. In Chapter 4, I shared with you my story about a thief who had a significant lottery win; she quickly wrote a check for the entire amount stolen. In another situation we were involved with, the thief was the daughter of the town's mayor, and he was willing to make repayment to keep his daughter's name out of the newspaper. Many other thieves have some equity in their homes or access to some form of saving.

On the other hand, don't underestimate the ability of a thief to scrape together money in an attempt to avoid jail time. Even if their pockets are empty, their spouse, parents, friends, or rich uncle may come to their aid. They may have equity in their house or 401(k) savings that can be accessed. I have seen victims give up on this far too easily.

Don't forget that the amount you should be seeking here is the amount of your "loss." This amount includes not only the amount stolen but also any consequential damages (for example, interest or late charges if bills were not paid) and the costs of investigating what happened. Many insurance coverages limit their coverage to amounts stolen and do not cover these other costs, although there are exceptions. Like dental insurance, what property insurance covers is a contractual matter between you and your insurance company. However, the fact that insurance does not cover specific costs in no way impairs your ability to claim them from the thief once you have received your insurance payment and are determining your deficiency.

The Made Whole Doctrine

One question that many dentists have is what happens if you receive funds from your insurance company, and there is also some recovery from the embezzler. Does your insurance company get this money, or does it go to you?

Suppose that someone steals $100,000 from you, and you recover $25,000 from your insurance. The thief then makes a payment of $40,000. Does the insurance company take the first $25,000 of this amount, leaving you with $40,000 in total, or do you get to keep the entire $40,000, making your total recovery $65,000?

The Made Whole doctrine means that you keep all recovered funds until you have recovered the entirety of your losses. At one time, it was possible in most states for insurance contracts to override the Made Whole principle (replacing it with something known as Insurer Whole). However, most states have enacted provisions blocking enforceability of Insurer First clauses.

Suppose you are receiving an insurance payment for your loss, and the insurance company is asking you to sign something called a "subrogation". In that case, this normally means that the insurance company is attempting to step in front of you if any recovery is made from other sources. You should get some advice about how your state treats Insurer Whole agreements before signing.

Making a Settlement

Often either the thief or the victim will get the idea that making an arrangement to repay some or all of the stolen money is a good idea. And it may well be, but there are several issues involved with making such an arrangement.

The first issue is that making a settlement may negate any ability to make a claim against your employee dishonesty insurance. In principle, your insurance covers your "loss." We were recently involved with a case where the amount stolen was about $85,000. Our client (without the benefit of advice from his attorney or us) agreed to settle with the thief for $40,000, which the thief promptly paid. The client's thinking was that the $40,000 plus the $25,000 insurance coverage that the client maintained would come close to making him whole.

The client then received a sizeable shock when he realized that he had effectively negated his ability to make an insurance claim by settling. The settlement's legal effect was to forgive the remaining $45,000 of the amount that was originally owed. At this point, the position taken by most insurance companies is that because the dentist agreed to reduce the amount owing to $40,000 and then received that amount, he had no "loss," and the Made Whole doctrine discussed previously would not protect him. Therefore, no amount was payable to him under that policy. Even though the client's *economic* loss was $45,000, the *legal* loss was nothing.

It is possible to recover funds from thieves in a way that preserves your ability to make an insurance claim, but it isn't a job for do-it-yourselfers.

The other danger when making a settlement is committing a crime called extortion, and it's easy to do. The next section provides some details.

The Extortion Trap

Some victims are quick to say that they will not prosecute a thief if full repayment is made. This discussion reflects a misunderstanding about how "prosecution" works that I will address later in this chapter. It also brings the victim dangerously close to committing a felony crime known as extortion (referred to as "blackmail" in some states).

When most people think of extortion, they think of what you see in the movies, where the loan shark threatens to break the legs of some unfortunate person unless they repay a gambling debt or money that was borrowed. Threatening someone with legal consequences unless they pay you a sum of money can also be extortion. In the words of attorney Mark Kennerly:

> "By and large, an attempt to obtain money from someone else by threatening to expose them or report them to the authorities arguably constitutes extortion or blackmail."[79]

---

[79] Kennerly, Max S. "When Does a Lawyer's Demand Letter Become Extortion?" Litigation & Trial, January 17, 2019. https://www.litigationandtrial.com/2013/07/articles/attorney/demand-letter-extortion/.

In *Plaintiff Magazine*, attorney David Cook said the following about extortion:

> "Extortion has been characterized as a paradoxical crime in that it criminalizes the making of threats that, in and of themselves, may not be illegal. In many blackmail cases the threat is to do something in itself perfectly legal, but that threat nevertheless becomes illegal when coupled with a demand for money."[80]

The handling of the question of repayment by a thief in exchange for your not taking action, whether initiated by the thief or by you, represents a huge potential legal quagmire. Committing a felony while trying to get your money back gives the embezzler leverage over the victim that I am certain you do not want to give. For this reason, these discussions should only take place with the benefit of legal advice. Normally, your attorney will require that all communication on this topic be done by them and in writing to ensure no potential for misunderstanding between the parties or straying into dangerous legal territory.

One of the services that Prosperident provides to victims is assistance with maximizing recovery. Please give us a call if this is something you wish to discuss.

---

[80] Cook, David. "Blackmail." *Plaintiff Magazine*, June 2013, www.plaintiffmagazine.com/recent-issues/item/blackmail.

Should I Report Them to the IRS?

Income gained through embezzlement is taxable just like any other income source, and reporting their ill-gotten gains to the IRS is not something that embezzlers typically do. I get asked by many victims whether reporting possible tax evasion on the embezzler part is something that they should do.

I think the answer really depends on the situation. If you are out of pocket and hope to recover the deficiency from the thief, introducing another creditor, who is going to jump in front of you in line immediately, may not be your best course of action. On the other hand, if you have recovered all that you are going to, and your motivation is to punish the embezzler, reporting them for tax evasion will certainly add to their misery.

Civil vs. Criminal Proceedings

Assuming that the thief is not willing to hand over money voluntarily, there are two avenues for you to obtain repayment. The first is to sue the thief, and the second is to seek a "restitution order" in the criminal proceeding that will occur.

You may know this already, but the legal system is effectively broken into two parts. Civil law, sometimes called "tort law," deals with disputes between citizens, whereas criminal law addresses conflicts between citizens and the state or federal government. There is a difference that is not intuitive. When someone commits a criminal offense, the law considers it a crime against all citizens of the jurisdiction. Therefore, the responsibility for, and cost of, obtaining justice are borne by the government and not the direct victim.

For example, if someone is stabbed (or embezzled) in your community, they are clearly a victim. However, criminal law is premised on the view that ultimately, all the citizens of your state lose from the offense because a crime impinges on their expectation of being able to live their lives with tranquility. The police and the prosecutorial service, which are both funded by taxpayers, assume the burden of bringing the criminal to justice.

In the United States, the "Dual Sovereignty Doctrine" gives both state and federal governments the power to pass their own laws and prosecute transgressions, except in areas where the Constitution reserves jurisdiction to one or the other. While violent crime is generally a matter of state jurisdiction, embezzlement is a crime that frequently transgresses both state and federal statutes. Depending on the situation, a prosecution may occur at either the state or federal level, or in rare cases, both jurisdictions.

Double Jeopardy

Part of the Fifth Amendment reads as follows: "nor shall any person be subject for the same offense to be twice put in jeopardy of life or limb."

There is a misconception that this "double jeopardy" provision precludes someone from being tried at both the state and federal levels or prevents a victim from seeking both civil and criminal remedies for the same action. Neither is correct.

The Constitution's Double Jeopardy Clause prevents multiple prosecutions or punishments for the same "offense."

Simultaneous state and federal prosecutions don't violate the clause because state and federal governments are separate sovereigns, each with their own set of criminal laws. Therefore, someone subject to simultaneous prosecutions is not being tried twice for the same offense. Similarly, a civil lawsuit does not have a sovereign (i.e., it is a dispute between two citizens), so the double jeopardy clause is not offended by a simultaneous criminal prosecution and lawsuit.

Who Pays for a Lawsuit?

In contrast to how the government funds the criminal justice system, because civil matters are deemed to be purely disputes between private citizens, the cost of litigation is borne completely by the parties. It is possible, but far from automatic, for the winner in a lawsuit to receive an "Attorney's Fee Award." If such an award is not granted, or if the lawsuit is unsuccessful, you will end up increasing the total loss from your embezzlement by the amount of your attorney fees.

But even if you win the lawsuit and are also awarded your attorney fees, here is the part you must understand: **winning in civil court is only beneficial if the embezzler pays you**. Let's say that you successfully sue your thief. If they do not pay you, you have **increased** the amount the embezzlement has cost you by the cost of your attorney's fees and other out of pocket costs of the lawsuit.

Judgments received in lawsuits go unpaid for two reasons; in some cases, the thief refuses to pay you, and in other situations, they simply do not have the means to pay.

Where someone chooses not to pay, enforcing the judgment requires further legal action on your part. You can garnish the thief's wages and seize bank accounts, but these steps take additional court appearances and incur more legal costs.

In the case where you are awarded a judgment against someone with a low or negative net worth, bankruptcy provides a way for them to "settle" their debts, usually with minimal adverse consequences to them. In bankruptcy, someone's non-exempt assets are liquidated, with the proceeds (after trustee fees) divided pro-rata among creditors. The average recovery by creditors in a consumer bankruptcy is about 15 cents per dollar owed.[81] This number might be optimistic for someone who has just lost a civil case that resulted in a significant judgment and is likely headed to prison, where earning potential is basically zero.[82]

Restitution Orders

Fortunately, there is a much better way to recover lost funds. When an embezzler faces criminal justice, it is customary for the judge, in addition to jail or whatever other penalties may be dispensed, to issue what is called a "restitution order."

[81]   Eraslan, Hülya, et al. "An Anatomy of U.S. Personal Bankruptcy Under Chapter 13." *International Economic Review*, John Wiley & Sons, Ltd (10.1111), 25 Aug. 2017, http://onlinelibrary.wiley.com/doi/abs/10.1111/iere.12231.

[82]   For an example of a thief discharging a debt through bankruptcy, see the story at https://www.prosperident.com/indiana-woman-husband-embezzle-247k-dentist-husband-tries-avoid-repayment-declaring-bankruptcy/.

In other words, as part of the sentence, the judge orders the thief to repay you. Suppose the embezzler has available assets like equity in a home. In that case, this can be forfeited, and any remaining balance can be addressed in monthly payments based on the thief's ability to pay (typically set at 25% of the thief's wages). I've even seen some judges get a bit creative with this and make the amount of jail time contingent on how much money is repaid. For example, one of our thieves was sentenced to 12 years in prison, but the sentence would be reduced to five years if the thief repaid $421,000 to the victim.[83]

Fines are also a possible punishment for embezzlement. The difference between restitution and fines is that restitution goes to the victim, whereas a fine belongs to the prosecution's jurisdiction.

A restitution order provides several advantages over the judgment you get if you win a lawsuit:

1. Unlike a victim obtaining a judgment in civil court, there is no cost to the victim to obtain a restitution order. The court only needs to know how much you lost, and this is information that you have already gathered for other purposes.

2. Your position is much better if the thief declares bankruptcy. In a bankruptcy, civil court judgments are lumped in with other debts, which, as discussed, are often satisfied for pennies on the dollar. In contrast,

---

[83]   See https://www.prosperident.com/prosperident-bags-another-one-office-manager-pleads-no-contest-to-embezzling-400k-from-roanoke-va-dental-practice/

restitution orders are excluded from bankruptcy and
still must be paid in full.

3. A law called the Employee Retirement Income Security
    Act of 1974 ("ERISA") protects specific retirement
    savings, for example, 401k plans, from seizure by
    creditors. However, ERISA does not protect these plans
    from seizure through a restitution order. A restitution
    order gives you access to assets that you would not
    have when enforcing a judgment from a civil court.

For these reasons, it is always better to obtain repayment
as a byproduct of the criminal justice system than to sue an
embezzler in civil court. While the granting of restitution orders
in criminal cases involving embezzlement should be automatic,
it is an excellent idea to maintain contact with the prosecuting
attorney to ensure that he or she is aware of your loss and that
you are looking for a restitution order.

Stolen checks

A third possible repayment source exists if an embezzler
stole checks from patients or insurance companies and cashed
or deposited them. The mechanism by which you can recover is
not intuitive but can often provide an excellent recovery source.

As long as you had not endorsed the stolen checks before
your thief took them, whoever issued them to you has not
adequately discharged their obligation of payment to you.

So, suppose an embezzler forges an endorsement on a
$1,000 check payable to you from an insurance company and

cashes it. In that case, you are entitled to demand another payment from the insurance company. The insurance company, in turn, can make a claim against its bank for allowing an improperly negotiated check to be paid.

Pursuing this is not a difficult decision in the case of stolen insurance checks. However, if checks from patients have been stolen, most practice owners are reluctant to make the patients pay a second time and then chase their bank for reimbursement. Fortunately, embezzlers are much quicker to steal institutional checks than those from patients.

Is the Embezzler's Spouse Liable?

One other consideration is whether the thief put money into purposes that benefited his or her spouse. For example, suppose stolen funds were used to make mortgage payments on jointly held property. In that case, this creates at least the theoretical possibility that you can go after the spouse's property as well.

There are a couple of practical issues. First, as discussed, suing embezzlers tends to be unproductive, and suing their spouses may be even more so, particularly as tracing specific funds to specific uses can get challenging.

Second, in many cases, the embezzler's spouse was unaware of the illegal activity. For many dentists, it seems unfair to embroil the embezzler's spouse in something about which they knew nothing.

What do I Tell People?

The question of what to tell various interested parties, including other staff members, patients who notice that a long-serving staff member has suddenly disappeared, referral sources if you are a specialist, and prospective employers looking for a job reference on the embezzler can be a challenging question. Unfortunately, this is not a question to which there is a "one size fits all" answer.

There are, however, a few principles that can help:

- What you tell your staff is largely determined by what they already know. In some situations, particularly where embezzlement was uncovered by another staff member, dancing around the topic may be ill-advised. However, if staff are unaware of what happened, you can simply describe the reason for someone's departure as an "integrity issue" and not be more specific. This comment could mean almost anything.
- If what staff already know renders the integrity explanation inadequate, possible, keep it non-accusatory. "We found some recordkeeping irregularities" or "there was money that was unaccounted for" should be used and not "Harold embezzled from us." In other words, it should be Harold's failure to keep good records that got him fired.
- Remember that anyone asking about what happened has some concerns of their own, and asking what happened to Harold is really their way of expressing

their concerns. Your ability to understand the "question behind the question" largely determines how successful at providing an answer that satisfies the questioner. In the case of an employee, the obvious concerns are whether they will be fired next, and if they know that embezzlement took place, whether it will mean that the office will close due to the losses suffered.

- When patients ask, the concerns are a bit different. If it is simply wondering how that long-term employee vanished, the answer should simply be that "we do not discuss personnel matters." If a patient is aware that something untoward happened, they may be wondering if somehow personal information was compromised. This is unlikely in embezzlement, but we can't expect them to know that.
- If you own a referral-based practice, one thing you need to be worried about is whether your departed employee gets a job with someone who refers patients to you. Simply making a statement to these doctors that Harold is not with you any longer but under no circumstance would be eligible for re-hire should give these important people sufficient warning.

Chapter 24 discussed giving a negative reference when you get calls from prospective employers.

29

Crime and Punishment

Unfortunately, far too many embezzlers are allowed to walk away from their crimes. One of the justifications that I often hear from dentists is along the lines of "the justice system won't punish them anyway."

While I am a critic of many facets of the justice system, for the most part, it does its job. People who embezzle from you may or may not go to prison. Their disposition depends on the amount stolen, the state where the crime took place, and whether there are mitigating factors that warrant a reduced punishment. However, at a minimum, a prosecuted embezzler will end up with a criminal record that will follow them around for many years, a fair amount of scorn from friends and family, a restitution order that is like a financial millstone around their neck, and hopefully a place on Prosperident's Hall of Shame. They will also normally need to pay for an attorney to defend them or rely on an overworked public defender to protect their interest.

What Law Does Embezzlement Break?

Most embezzlement is prosecuted under state law. I'll discuss federal prosecution in a subsequent section of this chapter.

In some states, embezzlement is a specifically identified offense; in others, it is dealt with as a more generic crime, often referred to as "fraud" or the even broader "theft."

There is also a legal distinction between embezzlement and something called "larceny." Larceny is the unlawful taking of someone else's property. Embezzlement is the unlawful taking of someone else's property *entrusted to the person who took it.*

Here is a simple example. If a staff member removes $20 from a dentist's purse while it sits in the doctor's private office, that is larceny. If a dentist asks a staff member to hold her purse while she goes to the gym, and the staff member removes $20, that is embezzlement because the thief was entrusted with the purse.

There was a time when many states treated embezzlement and larceny as separate offenses; with the predictable result that some offenders would escape punishment because they committed one crime but were charged with the other. Lawmakers have identified this loophole and have addressed it by creating a "merged" offense covering both embezzlement and larceny that prevents such maddening events.

For example, Section 484 of the California Penal Code includes the following:

> Every person who shall feloniously steal, take, carry, lead, or drive away the personal property of another, or who shall fraudulently

appropriate property which has been entrusted to him or her, or who shall knowingly and designedly, by any false or fraudulent representation or pretense, defraud any other person of money, labor or real or personal property … is guilty of theft.[84]

States have typically created a "graduated" system of offenses, where taking small amounts is classified as a misdemeanor crime, whereas larger amounts progressively become more serious felonies.

Using Illinois as an example,

- Misdemeanor embezzlement involves an amount less than $500, and the maximum penalty is one year in prison and a fine of $2,500.
- Stealing between $500 and $10,000 is a Class 3 Felony, punishable by two to five years in prison and fines of up to $25,000.
- Embezzling between $10,000 and $100,000 is a Class 2 felony, leading to three to seven years of imprisonment and a fine of up to $25,000.
- Embezzlement of property valued between $100,001 and $500,000 is a Class 1 felony, with a punishment of six to 30 years in prison and a fine of up to $25,000.

---

[84] California Penal Code, Section 484, California Legislative Information, https://leginfo.legislature.ca.gov/faces/codes_displaySection.xhtml?sectionNum=484.&lawCode=PEN retrieved August 29, 2020

- Embezzlement of property valued between $500,001 and $999,999 is a Class 1 non-probational felony, leading to four to 15 years imprisonment and a fine of up to $25,000.
- Embezzlement of property valued above $1 million is a Class X felony, leading to six to 30 years imprisonment and/or a fine of up to $25,000.[85]

Is Embezzlement Also a Federal Crime?

Yes, it can be. In the United States, the "Dual Sovereignty Doctrine" gives both state and federal governments the power to pass their own laws and prosecute transgressions, except in areas where the Constitution reserves jurisdiction to one or the other. While violent crime is generally a matter of state jurisdiction, embezzlement is a crime that frequently transgresses both state and federal statutes. Depending on the situation, a prosecution may occur at either the state or federal level, or in rare cases, both jurisdictions.

Many embezzlement patterns contravene federal laws. The most common federal laws are Wire Fraud (18 U.S.C. § 1343) and Mail Fraud (under 18 U.S.C. § 1341).

---

[85]   Illinois Embezzlement Charges & Penalties, Federalcharges.com https://www.federalcharges.com/illinois-embezzlement-laws/, retrieved August 6, 2020

Wire Fraud

The definition of wire fraud is rather broad and includes any writings, signs, signals, pictures, or sounds transmitted by wire, radio, or television in interstate or foreign commerce. The legal definition of wire fraud has four elements:

- The defendant created or participated in a scheme to defraud another out of money or property.
- The defendant did so with the intent to defraud.
- It was reasonably foreseeable that the defendant would use wire communications; and
- The defendant did, in fact, use interstate wire communications.

Mail Fraud

A person commits mail fraud when the scheme involves the mailing of something associated with the fraud. Mailing contracts, receipts, and communications regarding a fraudulent deal could all meet the law's requirements. The communications are not limited to the United States Postal Service. It can include mail sent through private and commercial interstate carriers, but the law does not require the communication to be from one state to another.

Racketeer Influenced and Corrupt Organizations

A third possibility for federal prosecution is the Racketeer Influenced and Corrupt Organizations (RICO) Act. Under RICO, a person who has committed "at least two acts of racketeering activity" drawn from a list of 35 crimes—27 federal crimes and eight state crimes—within a 10-year period can be charged with racketeering. RICO is a broad statute and has been applied to embezzlement situations occasionally, although its more customary usage is when there is a conspiracy involving multiple people.

Will the Federal Government Take My Case?

The Federal government annually prosecutes approximately only about 6,000 white-collar crimes. State statistics are a bit elusive, but state courts hear more than 90% of all criminal matters. So, embezzlement will normally need something noteworthy (usually big dollars involved) before the FBI or another Federal agency (the US Secret Service, possibly – the USSS and FBI jurisdictions overlap somewhat in this area) take an interest. I've heard various dollar thresholds quoted as to the amount that embezzlement must reach before a federal agency will get involved, with amounts between $100,000 and $250,000 as being the minimum. There is probably some variability depending on the local field office's caseload, so there may be validity to both numbers.

Federal agencies typically have more resources than their state or local counterparts. Also, the punishments for the federal crimes outlined above can be much stiffer than what is possible for state offenses. For example, both wire fraud and mail fraud carry maximum penalties of 20 years in prison plus fines of $250,000,[86] typically twice the jail time and ten times the fines that most state statutes permit.

Dealing with the Police and Prosecutors

Fortunately, most of us have relatively little experience dealing with the justice system, and when it becomes time to interact with it, find this system arcane and intimidating. The following is some information that may help you in dealing with the prosecutors and police:

1. It moves slowly.

    Many dentists have the mental image of calling the police and having the suspect taken away from their practice in handcuffs. This picture is not typically how it works. It is not like shoplifting, where the thief is generally caught with unpaid store merchandise outside the store. Catching someone "red-handed" is rare in embezzlement.

    It usually takes **years** for someone who embezzles from you to get convicted. Police and prosecutorial agencies are bureaucracies with limited budgets, and they are generally overworked. They must allocate

---

[86]   https://www.law.cornell.edu/uscode/text/18/1343 retrieved August 6, 2020

their resources between violent crime, which most citizens consider to be the priority, and economic crime. Because violent crime is more sensational than white-collar crime (we have all heard the news axiom that "if it bleeds, it leads"), it tends to be the priority of law enforcement.

However, like any bureaucracy, "the squeaky wheel gets the grease." The best way to keep your case moving forward is to ensure regular contact with the authorities. If you do not do this, they will shift their attention to whatever else is clamoring for their consideration.

2. It moves cautiously.

In criminal justice, there is a deeply ingrained concept called "Blackstone's Ratio" that states that it is better to allow ten guilty people to go free than to convict one person wrongfully.[87] Accordingly, this creates a conservative bias on the justice system's part to err on the side of caution and respect the accused's constitutional rights. Societally it makes good sense, but this bias can be maddening when you are a victim. It can be even more maddening when this bias or a violation of someone's constitutional rights results in a person who is obviously guilty going free.

For example, when police obtain evidence without a proper search warrant, or if a thief confesses to

---

[87] Blackstone, William. *Commentaries on the Laws of England.* 1st ed., 1765.

police but without being given the "Miranda" warning advising him or her of their Fifth Amendment rights and their ability to have an attorney present, normally the evidence acquired will be deemed to be inadmissible in court for the purpose of prosecution.

3. Victims cannot charge someone with a crime.

I hear many victims say that they want to "press charges." That is not exactly how the system works. Taking people to task for criminal acts is the responsibility of the government, not the victim. The victim's role is really to make the authorities aware of the crime, and then, in theory, the justice system should take over.

Charging someone with a crime is the District Attorney's responsibility, for crimes violating state law, or the US Attorney, for federal offenses. Laying a charge is often done at the request of a law enforcement agency; local or state police for state crimes, and usually, the FBI for embezzlement prosecuted under federal law.

Before an accused is charged with a federal felony, there is a requirement for a hearing by a "grand jury" made up of citizens to determine if there is sufficient basis to lay charges. This hearing is done *ex parte,* in other words, without the suspect being present or even aware of the hearing. Twenty-two states similarly require grand jury hearings for various charges.[88]

---

[88]   "How Does a Grand Jury Work?" *Findlaw,* criminal.findlaw.com/criminal-procedure/how-does-a-grand-jury-work.html.

4. Particularly if your evidence is "direct," as opposed to "circumstantial," you may be able to skip the police and go straight to the district attorney or U.S. Attorney. A direct approach to the prosecutor can considerably speed up the process but means that whatever additional evidence the police could have gathered is foregone.

Direct evidence shows both that the money is missing and that a particular person took it. An example of direct evidence is a staff member depositing an insurance check payable to you in their own account. Circumstantial evidence would be the deletion of a cash payment in your practice management software; this points to money missing but does not establish who took it (a staff member could have been using someone else's login information, for example).

While people do get convicted of embezzlement based solely on circumstantial evidence, a conviction is always easier if direct evidence can be obtained, and the police may have a role to play in filling any evidentiary gap that exists.

Police have a couple of investigative avenues that are not available to non-governmental investigators like Prosperident. First, a suspect really cannot refuse a request from police to be questioned. However, the suspect can insist on having legal representation for that questioning and can refuse to answer questions by asserting his or her Fifth Amendment right against self-incrimination. A private investigator can request that a suspect submits to questioning, but compliance is purely voluntary.

Second, given sufficient probable cause, police can obtain a search warrant, allowing them to search in places such as a suspect's house or vehicle, or they may compel records such as those from a bank account or credit card statement. Private investigators have no comparable ability. Being able to match missing funds with deposits in a suspect's bank account is an example of how a police investigation can upgrade evidence from circumstantial to direct.

Suppose you consider the evidence you hold to be compelling and reasonably complete. In that case, you have the option of placing that evidence in front of the district attorney and asking them to bring forward charges. A written report from a qualified investigator is often considered sufficient evidence for this approach.

If your circumstances allow you to skip over involving the police, doing so will significantly accelerate the process.

Your investigator should assist you in evaluating the evidence you have and the best way to move your matter forward. The good news is that there is a sense of closure in recovering funds and getting their matter addressed by the judicial system for most victims.

Sentencing

Keep in mind that all the prison terms referred to in this chapter are maximums. Many offenders will receive less than the maximum sentences, and some may receive house arrest or even a "suspended" sentence.

Many factors go into a judge's determination of the prison time to which an offender is sentenced. Some of these factors include:

- Is this a first offense, or is the thief a habitual criminal?
- How much money was stolen, over what period, and how "calculating" (i.e., deceptive) was the theft?
- While this probably should not be a consideration, often it is. How crowded is the jurisdiction's prison system?
- Has any restitution been made by the thief to the victim? Making even full restitution doesn't change the fact that a crime was committed, but it will normally reduce what would otherwise be the sentence considerably.
- Are there any "mitigating" factors? These can include the thief's age and health, a diagnosed mental illness, the judge's perception of how remorseful the thief is, etc.

Unfortunately, some of the mitigating factors are subjective. Remorse is easy to display, although, in my view, the remorse of many thieves is about being caught more than for whatever financial and emotional damage they may have caused.

Mental illness is also relatively easy to embellish. One mental condition diagnosed with some frequency these days is Post Traumatic Stress Disorder, often abbreviated as PTSD.

Studies suggest that approximately 7% of the population suffers from PTSD, with women being more likely to be afflicted than men.[89] I'm a military veteran and understand the impact that traumatic events can have on people, and I would never trivialize this debilitating phenomenon. However, unlike dental or other physical diseases, which have observable and measurable characteristics, PTSD's symptoms are all self-reported.

If I thought that a PTSD diagnosis would benefit me (like, for example, helping me avoid a prison sentence), I would do research using that amazing medical tool, "Dr. Internet," and then appear at my physician's office ready to recite a series of symptoms totally consistent with PTSD. I'm confident I would leave the physician's office with a diagnosis in my hand.

Unfortunately, using techniques like a phantom psychological disorder, people who understand how the system works can sometimes lighten their sentences. However, eventually, it tends to catch up with them.

But They Never Serve Their Full Sentence...

I often hear frustration expressed around how most thieves are released from prison after serving much less than their sentence. While I can understand the frustration, the parole system, while not perfect, is well thought out.

Society has a couple of objectives for people who are incarcerated; we want them to behave while in prison, and we want them to reintegrate into society when released. There

---

[89] The National Comorbidity Survey Replication, https://www.ptsd.va.gov/professional/treat/essentials/epidemiology.asp retrieved August 6, 2020

are relatively few tools available to encourage these things. We can't move them to a room with a balcony overlooking the pool or get them better food. What society can do is shorten their sentences if they do what they are supposed to, which is the parole system.

White-collar criminals tend to be model prisoners, and in general, will expect to be released at their earliest eligibility. This fact is well known to the judges who do the sentencing and is one factor they invariably consider.

Normally parole carries with it some conditions. Many of them are generic such as to "refrain from consuming drugs or alcohol" and "be of good behavior," Some conditions may be tailored to the situation and prevent the parolee from working in a dental practice or being in a position of handling money. They may also be subjected to monitoring, such as wearing an ankle bracelet.

A breach of parole conditions normally results in the parole being revoked, which means going back to prison to serve the balance of the sentence.

Despite all these measures, the probability of recidivism is high for all types of crime and noticeably higher for white-collar crime than it is for violent crime, as shown in the following chart.[90]

---

[90] White Collar Crime: Recidivism, Deterrence, and Social Impact Katie A Fredericks, Rima E McComas, Georgie Ann Weatherby, • Psychology • Forensic Research & Criminology International Journal 2016

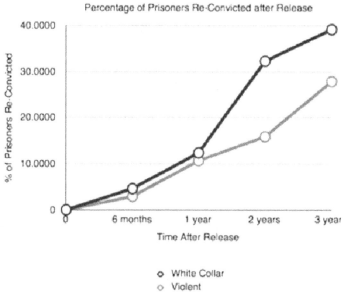

Figure 8 – Recidivism Probabilities - White Collar vs. Violent Crime

My Ex-employee has Offered to do a Lie-detector Test.

Polygraphy was once used far more than it is now. Its scientific basis has been widely debunked, and polygraph tests are no longer admissible as evidence in most court proceedings. Most states either ban polygraphs outright or limit their introduction to where doing so is agreed to by both prosecution and defense.[91] The Employee Polygraph Protection Act prohibits

---

[91]   What is a Polygraph Test? https://www.legalmatch.com/law-library/article/admissability-of-polygraph-tests-in-court.html

most private employers from using lie detector tests, either for pre-employment screening or during employment.[92]

Why have lie detector tests fallen out of favor? Because contrary to their name, the machines do not detect whether someone is lying. All that they can do is to measure involuntary physiological responses, such as perspiration and increases in respiration and heart rate, which are commonly associated with nervousness caused by lying. This limitation poses a couple of other challenges. First, an accused person may be nervous for other reasons (such as, for example, being hooked up to this strange machine in a room full of people after being falsely accused of a crime).

There is also a hypothesis that many sociopaths can beat a lie detector test. The psychological literature on this is somewhat divided,[93] but many behaviorists acknowledge the possibility that certain people do not experience strong physiological reactions when lying.[94]

---

[92] Employee Polygraph Protection Act, US Department of Labor https://www.dol.gov/agencies/whd/polygraph

[93] See, for example, Can a Psychopath or a Pathological Liar Pass a Polygraph Test? https://liedetectors-uk.com/can-a-psychopath-or-a-pathological-liar-pass-a-polygraph-test/

[94] The polygraph in doubt, American Psychological Association, July/August 2004, Vol 35, No. 7, Page 71

30

Trust, Then Verify: Systems That Win

By now, you know that embezzlement will eventually strike most practicing dentists and that amounts stolen can be significant.

There are a couple of things about this crime that surprises most of the dentists with whom I speak. First, when I bring up this topic with a dentist, typically, what is in his or her mind is cash theft. And while cash is the first target of most embezzlers, the amount of cash that most practices receive is small, and the long-term trend is downward.

For most embezzlers to steal the amounts that they think they should, they need to evolve beyond taking cash and into targeting other forms of wealth transfer. Cashing checks payable to you or the practice, hijacking credit card payments made to the practice, and intercepting direct deposits from insurance companies are all possibilities that are within the grasp of most thieves. The increasing level of automation in the banking system, and other technological innovations like e-deposits and devices that allow a smartphone to accept credit card payments, all play squarely into the hands of embezzlers who wish to progress beyond stealing $20 bills.

The second area of surprise for most dentists is the interactive nature of this crime, embezzlers' ability to evaluate the systems in place in an office, and to determine how to overcome or bypass those systems and the ability to adapt if control systems change.

Many dentists start with a distorted view of embezzlement. They believe, and this belief has been reinforced by some of the dental literature, that the people who work for them are not particularly smart. Therefore, they think that blocking specific embezzlement methodologies is the key to protecting themselves. So, they have been told, for example, that the practice owner should make bank deposits personally because doing so will thwart a would-be thief from stealing money from deposits.

I have seen many dentists learn the hard way that underestimating the creativity and determination of their adversary in this battle can be costly.

Thieves will adapt. The most common adaptation if the practice owner makes the bank deposits is to manipulate the practice management software into underreporting the amount received by the practice. Many practice owners believe that what is reported by their practice management software must be accurate, and this is not necessarily true.

There are lots of potential options for an embezzler. Over the years, my team and I have seen hundreds of different methodologies employed. Ultimately, this large number of options is what dooms the "denial of opportunity" strategies – embezzlers have too many possibilities for you ever to block them all. Taking a look through the Hall of Shame portion of our website at https://www.prosperident.com/category/hall-of-shame/ will give you an idea of the large number of possible methodologies available to an embezzler.

If the options available to a thief exceed your ability to block them, is this problem hopeless? Not at all. However, we need to shift our focus from blocking specific embezzlement methodologies to something more broad-minded.

Embezzlement consists of two elements, the act of stealing and then concealment of the theft. Stealing happens quickly and at a time and place chosen by the thief. Because of its fleeting nature, stealing is rarely observed by a dentist. However, the act of concealment tends to leave a permanent record, and therefore far easier to find. Later in this chapter, I will share some things for which to look.

The Question I am Asked Most Often

People attend my presentations for many reasons. Some want CE credit; others with embezzlement concerns are looking for information, and there are probably a few who are seeking entertainment.

There is also the group I call "validators;" these attendees come looking for an affirmation that they are doing the right things to address the possibility of embezzlement in their practices.

So, after the lecture or during a break, they will approach me to ask if a specific business practice (that they are using or are contemplating using) will "prevent" embezzlement. Some of the more common tactics discussed are constraining user privileges in their practice management software, separation of front-desk functions, direct deposit of insurance payments into their bank account, not accepting assignment of insurance benefits, and having a bank "lockbox" where incoming payments are directed and opened by a third party.

I think that most of them leave the conversation disappointed when I tell them that, while none of these things are bad ideas, at the same time, they are not likely to have any impact on embezzlement.

The reason is simple — each of these things removes one (narrow) opportunity for stealing. What none of them do is to address the thief's desire to steal, which is an incredibly strong force (and one that humankind has had little success in influencing despite much trying). A thief who knows you well, and probably understands your practice management software far better than you do, is very likely to overcome whatever obstacles you place in their path and successfully embezzle.

So, while I will never encourage you to stop looking for more streamlined ways to run your practice, we also cannot ever be lulled into thinking that we have created a structure that is embezzlement-proof.

So, if you are one of those unfortunates who has been on the receiving end of one of my "if you did that, here is how I would embezzle from you" sentences in one of my presentations, I apologize for leaving you feeling a bit deflated. However, I hope that you gained some insight that will equip you better to recognize and deal with the possibility of embezzlement in your practice.

How to Defeat Embezzlers

The following series of steps are designed to maximize your chances of finding concealments and some of the behavioral indications of embezzlement. I have mentioned a few of these already, but here is a review of the steps I would like you to follow:

1. The daily and monthly reports from your practice management software you review should be ones you have printed yourself. Allowing a staff member to generate reports for you created the possibility of "selective reporting," where you are looking at a subset of the practice's transactions while concurrently believing that you see the entire practice. Once you have reviewed a report, put your initials on it to confirm that it is the one you saw, and store it under lock and key for at least a year.

2. In Chapter 17, we mentioned the concept of articulation, where the day-end reports from your software need to total accurately to the month-end report. Confirming articulation will allow you to detect if someone is processing payments on a day when the office is closed.

3. Follow the day-end and month-end routines mentioned in Chapter 17 religiously. If you find that doing so takes more time than you have available, consider outsourcing (as opposed to delegating) the pure arithmetic functions of comparing deposits versus collections and articulation.

4. Have all statements you receive by mail, such as your bank statement, credit card statements for office credit cards, merchant terminal statement (from the machine in the office that accepts credit card payments) sent to your home instead of your office. Let's ensure that you see these first and create a level of mystery about what you do with them.

5. Monthly review the receivables report, with and without credits. We discussed the reasons for filtering credits out in Chapter 17. You should also compare individual past-due accounts from this month's report to last month's to monitor progress collecting past-due accounts and to ensure that older accounts were not written off without your knowledge.

6. Ensure that every staff member takes a vacation each year and ensure that most of it is taken all at once. Every staff member needs to be away from the practice for at least two consecutive weeks each year. If someone is embezzling, making them leave the practice for long enough that someone else must cover for them provides one of the best opportunities to realize that you have an embezzlement issue. I remember one large embezzlement that I investigated. It surfaced when the office manager broke her leg skiing one weekend and was not in the office on Monday for the first time in anyone's memory. A few hours later, one of the receptionists took the dentist aside to say that there was "something weird happening because I've gotten three of these very strange phone calls this

morning." These were calls that the office manager would normally have "handled" if she were there, but her absence meant that the calls went to someone else.

7. We discussed rules for dividing duties between your team in Chapter 20.

8. Have a written anti-fraud policy that clearly spells out what is fraudulent conduct. We are happy to supply a template if you want one.

9. Insist on cross-training of staff so that someone can provide backup for every function performed by your front desk.

These nine steps will not take a lot of your time but will dramatically increase your chances of spotting embezzlement in your practice quickly.

Behavior is The Key

I have mentioned my frustration with "dabblers" who do not let their incomplete knowledge about embezzlement stop them from dispensing advice. You can find these dabblers almost anywhere – internet chat forums, print or online articles, and even as conference speakers.

Here is one thing that they miss – far more embezzlement in dental practices is discovered because of behavioral abnormalities than financial ones. Several times, I have referenced a survey by the American Dental Association of embezzlement victims conducted in 2007. One of the questions that the surveyed victims were asked is what prompted the discovery of the embezzlement. Naturally, there was a broad spectrum of answers ranging from day sheets, not balancing to bank deposits (5%) to employees working unsupervised overtime (11%).[95] A few years ago, I had the idea that there was a better way to present the ADA's results. I categorized the responses as either "financial" or "behavioral." The day-ends not balancing would be an example of a financial irregularity, whereas the employee working unusual hours is a behavioral anomaly.

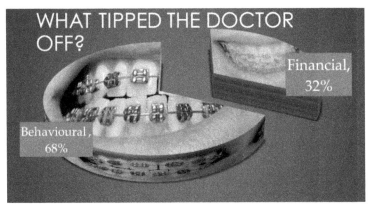

Figure 9 – Analysis of the 2007 ADA Embezzlement Survey

When I did this, something interesting was revealed. Less than one-third of the embezzlement discoveries in the survey

---

[95]   "2007 Survey of Current Issues in Dentistry - Employee Termination and Embezzlement - Download (SC) - SCID2-2007D." American Dental Association. 2007. Accessed July 30, 2019. http://ebusiness.ada.org/productcatalog/1668/Dental-Issues/2007-Survey-of-Current-Issues-in-Dentistry-Employee-Terminat/SCID2-2007D.

were prompted by a financial issue, with 68% of embezzlements coming to light because of how an employee was acting. This revelation about how dentists discover embezzlement is consistent with information from the Association of Certified Fraud Examiners, who have determined that more than 90% of embezzlers exhibit at least one behavioral characteristic of embezzlement.[96]

Almost without exception, the dabblers try to turn dentists into untrained (and uncompensated) internal auditors in their practices. Often their encouragement is platitudinous; they want you to "get more involved in the numbers," "implement checks and balances," and review many pages of reports. Furthermore, you should make the bank deposit yourself, lock up the checkbook, and the list goes on and on.

I think every dentist needs to review his or her day sheets ritualistically, and I would never discourage any dentist from being involved and aware of their practice's finances. But since you have a finite amount of time to devote to protecting yourself from embezzlement, I will tell you categorically that this time will be better spent watching staff behavior than it ever would trying to count the pennies.

The activity that you can do that probably has the highest payoff in terms of the ratio of time spent to the possibility of detecting embezzlement is to review the alarm company's access log, which will tell you if any staff members are working at unexpected times.

---

[96]   "2016 ACFE Report to the Nations." *2016 ACFE Report to the Nations*, www.acfe.com/rttn2016/perpetrators/red-flags.aspx.

Some of the behavioral markers of embezzlement are listed in this table:

	Behavior	Description	Prevalence in the 2019 ADA Center for Dental Practice Report
1.	Does not offer transparency.	Embezzlers may bristle when asked for an explanation of something, may give an obfuscatory explanation, or may be defensive when questioned. They may have an undertone or even a verbalization that it bothers them that, after all that they do, you don't appear to trust them.	42.00%
2.	Displays extreme territoriality about duties.	It is common for these people to create a belief on the part of the practice owner that he or she is free to focus on clinical practice, believing that the administration of the practice is under the firm control of the thief.	29.75%
3.	Protective of workspace.	This protectionism may also extend to someone touching "their" computer.	28.53%
4.	They are often "blamers".	Often will refuse to accept responsibility for anything that has gone wrong. The blame might be directed at other staff or third parties like the company making your practice management software or an insurance company. They may bully other staff, and other staff may be reluctant to work with them.	21.17%

5.	Tends to have a precarious existence.	Some live very much hand-to-mouth. They tend to be renters, not owners, move frequently, and may have creditors chasing them for money. Their willingness to cut corners will extend to other parts of their lives. This person may be someone who has declared bankruptcy multiple times or has a track record of being evicted. There may be calls to them at work from creditors. Others will show some stability but will clearly be living beyond their means.	20.86%
6.	Refuses to delegate duties or cross-train.	This refusal is territoriality's close cousin. Cross-training another employee in some part of their job creates the possibility that some part of their responsibilities gets reallocated, making embezzlement more difficult. Also, many embezzlers take comfort in knowing that some key "institutional knowledge" exists only inside their heads and would vanish if they leave the practice.	19.02%
7.	Wants "alone time" in the office.	Thieves typically want to be alone when they steal. Stealing takes concentration, and it is easier to do when the office is not filled with staff and patients. Superficially, working "for" you and working "against" you don't look that different, so when a thief comes in early or stays late, the doctor interprets this as an uncommon dedication to the job and doctor.	18.71%

8.	Refuses to take a vacation or takes it in small increments.	May also insists that his or her work be "held over" while he or she is away (in other words, not given to another person). As the discovery of the office manager, I mentioned earlier in the chapter as a result of her skiing accident, embezzlers know that they are particularly vulnerable when they are away from the office. As you might expect, these people seldom lose time due to being sick. Their willingness to drag themselves into the office when under the weather is also misinterpreted as hyper-dedication.	7.06%
9.	Offers strong resistance to change.	Resistance may extend to office procedures, banking arrangements, or other activities with financial implications.	Not a response category in the ADA survey
10.	Exerts considerable influence over the choices of advisors to the practice.	Many embezzlers will slowly replace many of the people who advise or provide services to the practice with their own "team." This influence may include everyone from the IT company used by the practice to the bank, the dental supply company, to even the accountant. These people are not necessarily complicit in theft. However, they all see their loyalty as belonging to the thief instead of you. For someone who is providing services to the practice only because of their relationship with the embezzler has a concern, they are far more likely to express that concern to the embezzler (who will explain it away) than to approach you.	Not a response category in the ADA survey

11.	Has resistance to upgrading to the most recent version of your practice management software.	They can also be unwilling to change to a different brand of software. An embezzler is normally fearful that change will impact one of the methodologies that they use to steal.	Not a response category in the ADA survey
12.	Displays opposition to you hiring a consultant, software trainer, or another external advisor.	Most embezzlers are confident that they can pull the wool over their doctor's eyes. But an outside advisor, who is not under the spell of the thief, and who thinks full-time about dentistry as a business, represents a much larger threat.	Not a response category in the ADA survey

There are many more behavioral telltales of embezzlement, but these represent the main ones. The key to recognizing embezzlement early is to become a better observer of staff behavior. I'll offer a few ways to do this. First, I see many doctors eating their lunch in the private office, with staff together in the staff room. I recognize that for many doctors, lunch is when they can return some emails and catch up on paperwork. Still, I'd suggest that, whenever possible, eating lunch with staff gives you an excellent chance to get to know them better (and of course, watch for certain behaviors).

Second, we have developed a tool to assist a practice owner in assessing the risk that they are victims. Prosperident's Embezzlement Risk Self-Assessment Questionnaire (ERAQ) was originally something that we developed for internal use but eventually decided to release publicly. This web-based questionnaire takes about 15 minutes to complete and allows you to compare the behavioral risk presented by a team member's actions to thousands of other practices. You can access and take our questionnaire, for a nominal fee, here: www.prosperident.com/store.

Performing the monitoring steps listed in this chapter and becoming a better observer of staff are the best things you can do to protect yourself. So, what are you waiting for?

31

How Does Prosperident Do Its Work?

Prosperident is a team of over 20 men and women who have spent a good part of their lives working in dentistry. Many have clinical backgrounds as dentists, hygienists, or dental assistants. Some have managerial experience as office managers, consultants, or software trainers. Add in a few with accounting backgrounds and experience as private investigators, and you have an eclectic group who live and breathe solving the crime of embezzlement in our narrow chosen field. Most have or are working towards a professional designation in fraud examination.

Investigations

Our work largely consists of pulling apart a practice's practice management software to discover what is buried within. Consistent with what I have said elsewhere in this book, our work is planned to be carried out in secret because, in many situations, the staff members we are investigating are still working in the practice.

To access practice management software and keep our work undetectable, our IT team will take a copy of the data files from the practice management software and then use those data files to construct what we call "forensic duplicates," which are working copies of practice management software that exist in our computer lab. Our investigators, who have job titles like Fraud Examiner or Senior Fraud Examiner, do all their work using these forensic duplicates and generally do not even log in once to the "live" software in your practice or in the cloud if you are using cloud software.

Working this way provides us with several advantages. It keeps our activity invisible to your staff. It prevents the disruption of your practice. And it allows us the luxury of working with data that will not change through the course of our work. When we look at a practice, we look at past transactions for a defined period (which is often a year but might be something different if the situation warrants). When you are doing this in live software, one thing that complicates this task is the ongoing transactions posted in the software over the time it takes to complete your work. While for you, this activity is a necessary part of your practice being in operation, for us, it would be "noise." Working with a cloned set of data eliminates the noise and gives us a much more stable platform with which to work.

What do we do with that data? Normally, our investigation follows two phases, and these closely follow the approach that most embezzlers take, as outlined in Chapter 21. We begin with a reconciliation phase, where we compare collections according to the practice management software with a practice's bank account, merchant account, and other deposit sources for the period that we are reviewing. The purpose of this is simple; we want to ensure that everything that the practice management software says was received made it to the practice's bank account.

In our second "concealment" phase, we intensely review the practice management software to look for the transactions people make when they want practice management software to misrepresent what really happened. What we look at varies a bit depending on the situation, but normally we are looking for about 20 types of fraudulent transactions.

Sometimes our examination involves looking at reports and ledgers in an office's practice management software. Most dentists do not have occasion to think of it this way, but your practice management software really consists of two parts. There is an interface, or "front end," and there is a relational database behind it. The interface is what gives you access to the data in a (hopefully) user-friendly way. However, it is not the only way to access the database.

We do make use of the interface to look at reports and individual patient ledgers. However, that approach can be confining because we are limited by the design choices made by the people who developed the practice management software. Increasingly, we export raw data from a practice's software into a spreadsheet, where we can manipulate and sort the data in ways that we could never do if we used the software's interface.

We start by identifying suspicious transactions and then set about determining whether, in fact, they were fraudulent. At the end of our process, we provide a detailed report and assist a victim with obtaining recovery and facilitating prosecution.

Protection

Prosperident's fastest growing segment is Office Protection System, where we proactively assist practice owners in perfecting their practice systems to lower their vulnerability to embezzlement. We assist practices on an individualized basis to ensure that their balancing and oversight processes are done properly, that people are properly screened before being hired, that their practice management software's security and user permissions are correctly established, that HR policies align with the goal of protecting the practice from embezzlement and review many other areas.

If you would like to speak with me about your practice, please give us a call at 888-398-2327 or connect through our website at www.prosperident.com.

32

You've Got This!

As I look back over the thirty years that I have worked with the dental profession, I cannot help but think how blessed I have been to be serving such a wonderful group of people. At a visceral level, the havoc that embezzlement wreaks against this noble profession angers me, and I hope to help you protect yourself by sharing what I have learned with you.

Let's start by accepting that thieves have several advantages in the battle between embezzler and dentist.

1. I know very few dentists who chose that career because they had a burning desire to be business owners. Most of the thousands of dentists I have had the privilege of meeting or working with think of being in business as the "necessary evil" that comes with practicing their cherished profession.

2. The pure and truthful way dentists relate to each other serves you well in the clinical environment. However, it can make you ill-equipped once you step outside the "clinical bubble" and encounter people who have hidden agendas and do not share your ethics.

3. The thief in your practice has far more time and energy to devote to solving the problem of separating you from your money than you can devote to protecting yourself.

4. Some of the behavioral manifestations of embezzlement make the thief outwardly appear like the ideal employee.

Is this, therefore, a hopeless cause? In other words, is embezzlement inevitable?

Actually, the tools available to you are powerful and effective if you recognize their existence and use them.

The starting point is understanding why people steal and how embezzlers think. I have given you plenty of information on these topics.

The other tool is the recognition that "prevention" is a fallacy and that your efforts should be focused instead on control via early detection.

This book has provided you with some simple yet necessary financial measures to employ in your practice. I have made a few suggestions about where outsourcing a certain number of them is probably a good idea. If you want more in-depth help in this area, please feel free to reach out to us.

You now know that observing employee behavior is the real key to detection and that an overwhelming majority of embezzlers "act like they are stealing."

You also understand the importance of acting decisively when embezzlement is suspected or confirmed.

So now that you are well-equipped to deal with embezzlers, what are you waiting for? Protect yourself!

Annex A

Checklist for Terminating an Employee

INSTRUCTIONS:
The following checklists will help guide you through the various actions to take when an employee leaves your practice.

Computer / Telephone Checklist – Employment Termination				
Item	Person Responsible (initials)	Check When Completed	Priority	Comments
Close personal computer accounts		☐		
Change password on all computer accounts (office email, Windows login, Practice Management Software, etc.)		☐		
If the employee had remote computer access, ensure that it is terminated immediately.		☐		

Search the employee's workstation and server for any web-based software giving remote access. This software could have names like LogMeIn, TeamViewer, goto myPC, Instant Housecall, etc. If in doubt, turn off the employee's workstation or disconnect from your network until the issue is resolved	☐		Remote access could allow a terminated employee to destroy files or even wipe the server's hard disk
If the automated telephone system mentions the employee by name, get announcements changed	☐		
Change the password on the employee's office email account. Keep the account open in case information that can be used as evidence arrives by email.	☐		
Change the access code on the employee's office voicemail account. Do not delete voicemail messages	☐		
Arrange for the website to be updated to remove references to the employee	☐		
Ensure that, if the employee was responsible for social media postings for the office, you regain control over the social media accounts.	☐		

Financial Checklist – Employment Termination				
Item	Person Responsible	Completed	Priority	Comments
Cancel any office credit cards that the employee may have had access to.		☐		
If using a payroll service, after the employee's final pay is prepared, ensure that the payroll service is aware that the employee has been terminated. If the employee had the authorization to deal with the payroll company, ensure that it is revoked.		☐		
If the employee had purchasing authorization with one or more suppliers, notify them that this authorization has been revoked.		☐		
Verify that all Petty Cash reimbursements for the employee are completed		☐		
Ensure that all federal and state termination documents are prepared		☐		
Cancel the employee's telephone authorization code		☐		

Office Property Checklist – Employment Termination				
Item	Person Responsible	Completed	Priority	Comments
Retrieve building and other keys		☐	1	
Ensure that the employee's alarm access code is removed. If a shared access code was being used for the alarm system, issue new individual codes to the employees, cleaners, etc.		☐	1	
Change locks on the door		☐	1	If you rent your premises, ask the Landlord to change the locks. **It is not enough to get the employee's key back because they may have other copies. CHANGE THE LOCK.**
Retrieve and/or disable electronic access cards		☐		
Retrieve ID cards, if required.		☐		

Retrieve the mailbox key if the employee has one. Arrange for the mailbox lock to be changed if the employee had access		☐	
Retrieve dosimeter		☐	
Retrieve any other office property		☐	
Verify that the employee has returned all property (e.g., cell phone, pagers, laptops, office-provided clothing, tools, equipment)		☐	
Ensure that the employee leaves all office reference materials (e.g., files, manuals, computer files)		☐	

Employment Termination Checklist				
Item	Person Responsible	Completed	Priority	Comments
If the employee has resigned, obtain a letter of resignation (or confirm oral resignation in writing). Otherwise, prepare a suspension or termination letter and have it on hand at the exit interview		☐		
Ensure completion of the employee's final timesheet/ record of employment.		☐		
Make the final paycheck available on the employee's last day of work. Include accumulated vacation pay and any other statutory entitlements in the final paycheck.		☐		
Schedule exit interview. If possible, avoid termination on a Friday. Try to schedule for the end of the day so that the terminated staff member is the only person left in the office.		☐		
Ensure that the employee's home address and phone number are correct so that employment documents will be mailed to the appropriate address.		☐		

Have a box or boxes ready for packing the employee's personal effects. Supervise the employee when he/she is cleaning out their desk. Do not let them touch any computer or office phone.	☐		
Escort the employee off the premises, ensuring that you have their key	☐		
Ensure that the employee has a safe ride home. They may be too upset to drive, and public transit may not be practical if they are carrying their effects. Offer to pay for a ride home. DO NOT DRIVE THEM HOME YOURSELF.	☐		
Communicate the departure of the employee to other staff.	☐		
If prospective employers call seeking a reference, limit response to providing dates of employment and answering the question, "Would you rehire this person?"	☐		
To prevent unintentional admission of the employee to your office by your cleaning staff or another outside service provider who may be in your office after hours, advise them that this person is no longer permitted to enter the premises.	☐		

Annex B

Panic Checklist for When Embezzlement is Suspected or Confirmed

Introduction

You are reading this checklist because you think you may be the victim of embezzlement. It's important to take the right steps.

Your objectives:

(1) **Minimize future losses**   (2) **Preserve evidence**   (3) **Maximize Recovery**

IMPORTANT FIRST STEPS:	WHY?
Act normally and keep your suspicions to yourself	The employee is looking at you each day to see if you are on to them.
Remember that stealth is paramount and that nothing should be done to alert staff that you have concerns	If a thief thinks they are about to get caught, they may do something desperate to try to avoid the consequences of their actions. This could include the destruction of records, and in rare cases, violent acts.
Make a complete backup of practice management software data and take it off-site	If you do not know how to do this, contact Prosperident or the practice management software manufacturer for guidance. **Do not involve staff.**
Recognize the need for specialized advice	Embezzlement investigation is not a "do-it-yourself" project for most dentists. Most CPA firms do not have all the tools they need to investigate dental embezzlement successfully. Investigating dental embezzlement requires knowledge of embezzlement methodologies, practice management software, and the way dentists interact with insurance companies. There are only a few companies in North America with significant experience in this.
Ensure communication with investigators is secure	Ensure that all telephone and email communications with your advisors are secure. Change email password or set up a new email address for this purpose.

DO NOT:	WHY?
✖ Blame yourself	Over 80% of dentists will be embezzlement victims in their careers. Embezzlement is not caused by dentists being unsophisticated in business matters or inattentive; it relates far more to the situation of the embezzler than the dentist.

Embezzlers are smart, desperate people and normally can easily circumvent the controls found in dental offices.

Also, no dentist loses their license over being an innocent victim of embezzlement |
✖ Contact police at this point	Police do not have the resources/expertise to be **primary** investigators here. They need someone with specific expertise to do that. Once the primary investigation is complete, the police will ensure that the law is applied.
✖ Contact any affected dental insurance companies yet	This contact is premature until a preliminary investigation is done and may prompt an unwelcome audit by the insurance company.
✖ Ask unusual questions of staff or to ask staff for extra reports	This will almost certainly tip off a hyperperceptive employee.
✖ Confront the employee	This is also premature. This can be effective later in the process, but some investigation needs to happen first
✖ Terminate an employee, even if you are "pretty sure"	Even in "employment at will" jurisdictions, many employees have a good basis for disputing their termination. It's fine to suspend a suspected employee, but don't fire them until you have consulted with experts.

✖	**Make any changes to banking arrangements, computer software (such as an upgrade to the latest software version), etc.**	These actions will arouse the suspicions of the thief and may complicate investigative efforts. Please be aware that it is the standing policy of many software companies to ask you to upgrade to the latest version if you call them for help. Be prepared to explain to them why this cannot be done in your situation.
✖	**Make or accept any offer to "settle".**	Making such an offer may constitute "extortion", which is a crime and may also result in your losing insurance benefits that you could have had.

How we can help:

- We conduct **stealthy** embezzlement investigations on behalf of dentists to determine if embezzlement is occurring.
- Prosperident only works with dentists.
- If embezzlement is found, we coordinate the remediation engagement and the activities of other parties including your attorney, CPA, police, your "employee dishonesty" insurance carrier, and affected dental insurance companies.
- Staff include former practicing dentists, CPAs, and people with backgrounds in consulting, practice management, and software trainers.
- Toll toll-free numbers (staffed 8:00 am to 8:00 pm Eastern time) is 888-398-2327.
- The priority embezzlement email address (monitored 365 days per year by duty investigator) is emergency@ dentalembezzlement.com.

- When contacting us by phone or email, please provide the following:
    - o A private email address. We will not send email to a generic address like "info@" or "office@"
    - o The best time for us to call back and a "safe" number to call – for security reasons we never call the general office number of a dentist; we need a cell phone or home number.
    - o Does the employee still work at the practice?
    - o What practice management software is currently in use? (Dentrix, Eaglesoft, Ortho2, Open Dental, etc.)

Printed in the USA
CPSIA information can be obtained
at www.ICGtesting.com
CBHW070329080324
5091CB00002B/3

9 781779 410153